Caught in the Middle

Caught in the Middle

A Leadership Guide for Partnership in the Workplace

Rick Maurer

Foreword by
John L. Mariotti
President & General Manager,
Huffy Bicycles

Publisher's Message
by Norman Bodek
President, Productivity, Inc.

Productivity Press
Cambridge, Massachusetts   Norwalk, Connecticut

Productivity Press, Inc.
P.O. Box 3007
Cambridge MA 02140
(617) 497-5146

Cover design by Russ Funkhouser
Printed and bound by Maple-Vail Book Manufacturing Group
Printed on acid-free paper in the United States of America

Library of Congress Cataloging-in-Publication Data

Maurer, Rick
    Caught in the middle : a leadership guide for partnership in the workplace / Rick Maurer.
        p.   cm.
    Includes bibliographical references and index.
    ISBN 1-56327-004-8
    1. Industrial management--Employee participation.   2. Leadership.
I. Title.
HD5650.M376   1992
658.4'092--dc20   91-23238
                                                                            CIP

92 93 94 10 9 8 7 6 5 4 3 2 1

Contents

Publisher's Message

How does it feel to be "caught in the middle"? More and more managers these days are finding out. Perhaps you're among them.

Middle managers are usually put in charge of planning effective ways to meet goals set by their bosses, then directing other people to carry them out. When a manager's performance is reviewed, the boss wants to see measurable results. It is the manager's responsibility to do whatever it takes to get those results from his or her reports.

Business is changing, and so are traditional work relationships. Top management recognizes the need for new approaches to keep the organization competitive. They've discovered a new truth (and it is a real one): These new approaches, including total quality management, just-in-time, and total productive maintenance, won't succeed without the participation of an informed and motivated work force.

It has become clear that front-line employees are a valuable but overlooked source of information about the company's own customers and processes. Competitors have discovered new value in their employees and are pulling ahead by using their creative ideas and giving them more responsibility.

In this age of corporate downsizing, middle managers' jobs depend on how well they deal with paradox:

- They must show that the company cares about people, but they may be required to lay people off.
- They must be committed to producing quality, yet are expected to order shortcuts, if necessary, to deliver the product on time.
- They must encourage employee achievement, but cannot invest time and resources in necessary training.

The manager's daily work is often a delicate dance between meeting corporate goals and maintaining credibility with the employees.

When top management gets religion and decrees, "Let There Be Employee Involvement," it doesn't always think about the implications for those who manage its newly empowered ranks. The recent move toward employee participation often increases a manager's sense that he or she is alone in the middle. The employees have new expectations of a sympathetic ear for their ideas, and the boss expects ever stronger results.

Most managers welcome the idea of a new partnership in the workplace. They know their people are brimming with thoughts about how things could be different and better, ideas that can help them meet that bottom line together. These managers are full of good intentions, but deeply uneasy about the process of altering their roles, sharing authority, trying to build an environment of trust. Most managers who are told to create employee participation naturally wonder, "How on earth can I change all that?"

Caught in the Middle is a book about where to start. It is a road map that can help middle managers find their way through the changes in employee management they will face in the years to come.

As a manager, you know that the transformation to participative management can't happen overnight; it is not a program-of-the-month that can be installed and forgotten. It is a process that requires commitment, one that asks you to reconsider your thinking about your employees as well as your daily interactions with them.

Caught in the Middle acknowledges the discomfort you may feel in exploring this wild and uncharted territory. It helps you recognize the signals, within yourself as well as around you, that will show you how to get where you need to go.

Rick Maurer developed this guide to the new territory through his experience in helping a number of companies and government organizations face the challenges of change. He devotes Part One to helping you understand the need for a partnership approach to management and comparing several options for bringing it about. One chapter, "Traveling the Road to Hell," describes major barriers that can block a shift to participative management (additional avoidable pitfalls are listed in later chapters in "Road to Hell" subsections).

Once you've got your bearings, you're ready for Part Two, "Getting Started." First on the agenda is understanding where you are in the process, using a self-assessment questionnaire and interpretation. As you use it, suppress your urge to say, "Boy, I wish the boss would take this quiz," and look candidly at your own current approach.

Subsequent chapters take you through the formation of a steering committee to assist you in moving toward a team approach, with additional assessment forms to shape the discussion. One important chapter focuses on the values that promote true participation. Finally, the book helps you chart a plan and put it in action.

Part Three is about keeping the vitality in the approach you've adopted. Sustaining teamwork over the long term will require you to develop the skills of your people and build their ability to shoulder delegated responsibility. Self-direction doesn't happen by telling your staff to manage themselves; to reach that level they need your guidance, support, and coordination of efforts. An important point to remember during this process is to encourage initiative rather than punishing the risk-takers.

Rick Maurer wraps his advice in language that is wonderfully easy to read and relate to. In his self-assessment forms, you will find valuable tools that help you evaluate your own situation. The forms are compiled separately in an appendix so that you can easily reproduce them for group discussion. A "Resources" appendix lists ample reading and viewing material for continuing your exploration of total employee involvement and quality.

Caught in the Middle is a book for you to read alone and pass out to your steering committee — and yes, you can give a copy to the boss.

We are grateful for the efforts of a number of people in producing this book, especially to the author for his openness and accessibility during the process. Our special appreciation to John Mariotti, President and General Manager of Huffy Bicycles, for an insightful foreword based on his experience with culture change at his company. Thanks to Bill Dickinson, editor of the *TEI Newsletter*, for first introducing Rick to us, and to acquisitions editor Karen Jones for persuading him to publish with us. Dorothy Lohmann managed the manuscript preparation, with assistance from Michelle Marchetti Coughlin, copyeditor; Phyllis Lindsay, proofreader; Maureen Murray and James Rolwing, word processors; and Jennifer Cross, indexer. Production was managed by David Lennon, with typesetting and art by Susan Cobb and Gayle Joyce. The cover was designed by Russell Funkhouser.

Norman Bodek
President
Productivity, Inc.

Foreword

I don't know if you found the title and concept of this book intriguing, but I certainly did. I read a lot of books and I often bog down about a third of the way through them — but not this one! There are so many books directed toward top management, and still more loaded with techniques, methods, and case histories about someone who did something outstanding. Unfortunately, few of them talk about the problems people encounter and even fewer provide the means for you and me to analyze and decide how to do what in our own companies.

At Huffy Bicycles, we have been working with our supervisors (we call them area coordinators now) for several years to help them develop into the right kind of managers for their role for the future. Unfortunately, we took them down several blind alleys and around more than a few wrong turns on the way. Only recently have we begun to really listen to them and involve them as we should have. Up until now, they were very definitely "caught in the middle."

Top management (me included) often develops "grand plans." Even when such a plan is a *good* plan, it frequently is only a skeleton; others in the organization are required to put the meat on the bones. In the process of getting our work force enthused, involved, and (hopefully someday) empowered and self-directed, we created large expectations in their minds. With the demise of the "old rules," which we have publicly declared no longer appropriate, there was an absence of "new rules." The work force needed some kind of rules because they needed structure in their environment. They needed to know how they should behave in this new world they found thrust upon them. It fell on middle management and particularly on first-line supervisors to figure out what the new rules should be, *while* they were trying to operate their departments and enforce the new rules. (Remember, we brought them up in an era when their job was at least partly that of a policeman and relatively little of a coach, a facilitator, or even a leader!)

In this book, Rick Maurer talks about many things that are important — he recalls the basics of human needs and effectively relates them to managers caught in the middle. He provides tough reminders to those of us in top management about our role and responsibility in the whole process of change. Maurer describes with amazing clarity situations that I have personally seen (and felt) as we attempted to move from an autocratic environment to one of (first) employee involvement, (then) employee empowerment, and (ultimately) self-directed teams.

What struck me as particularly different and useful about *Caught in the Middle* is that it reviews the options while charting the progression and the traps. To use an expression, it "nixes the quick fixes." Perhaps more important, it warns in advance about some of the problems. This is infinitely better than learning them the painful way — by running directly into them on the "road to hell."

The book includes some excellent and badly needed advice on "management-by-wandering-around," including ways to use this approach even when your staff is spread out at remote locations. There is a very important discussion about commitment to values, with some key insights on how to deal with fear, risk, and job security. One of the most thought-provoking parts of the book is entitled "Are We Ready for All This?" In order to help answer this question, a practical self-diagnosis tool is included, as well as a discussion tool that can aid in exposing problem areas objectively.

Maurer's refreshing mix of expressions — ranging from "walking the talk" and "grafting Japanese branches onto American

trees" to Peter Block's categories of "bedfellows" and "fence sitters" — create a clear vocabulary to describe the difficult challenges
for those who are "caught in the middle," and for their leaders in
top management.

This is a book that needs to be read with a notepad and pen
nearby. The use of the self-diagnosis tools and the "simple" questions that cry out to be answered provide both information and
self-assistance. Near the end of the book, I was struck particularly
by a significant point entitled "What Did the Boss Think?" How
many times does the boss *not show* his or her reaction, leaving
everyone wondering — and worrying?

Maurer is exactly right in his cautionary comments on trust.
In my experience, trust is one of the most difficult values to build
and the easiest to destroy. For those who are caught in the middle, it can be like a house of cards, unless there is a solid foundation and framework for it, based on the commitment of the
company's leaders.

In writing this foreword, I've reflected on some of the most
intriguing parts of this very special book. I hope my thoughts have
piqued your curiosity. As I read the book, I found myself drawn
deeper and deeper, making notes all the way. I have been living
and working with a group of people who are "caught in the middle"; the sooner I can help them grow and develop into their new
positions, the better their lives will be — and mine too. Hopefully
this book will be as much help to you as it was to me.

John L. Mariotti

Preface

My mother was so proud when I became a manager. What am I going to tell her now?

— A manager on learning that he was
no longer a manager but a facilitator

Congressman Morris Udall, speaking before a caucus late in the 1988 Democratic Convention, told the weary delegates, "Although everything's been said, not everyone's said it." I know how he felt. So many sound and sometimes eloquent books have been written on the subject of manager as leader. The recent proliferation is astounding. In 1989 Warren Bennis alone added two new titles to the growing list. Where will it all end? Obviously, not here.

In spite of the growing list (and I recommend some of my favorites at the end of this book), I believe little has been written for the supervisor and middle-level manager who is faced with the challenge of increasing participation within his or her work unit. One organization may call it employee involvement, another participatory management, others may not name it but encourage managers to just get people involved.

As organizations realize that those closest to the customer or product know the problems and possibilities best and rightly attempt to push staff involvement and control down to the lowest levels, they have failed to define precisely what the manager's role is in this process.

This book is written for those managers caught in the middle. It is written for those who want to create an environment that treats people (themselves included) with respect and dignity, and for managers and supervisors who wish for work in which they can take pride. I have visited and spoken with managers who are wrestling with these challenges to learn what works and what doesn't. Although no two stories are the same, there is a common body of practice that can offer managers a better map of this new terrain. Talk to managers and hourly workers at some General Electric plants, for example, and you hear hardened veterans of labor/management struggles speak with pride about "my company" and "my career." This is a far cry from the workplace that breeds automatons and work settings that cause workers to shrug and remark, "It's just a job."

But how do we open that door to job satisfaction and pride for the manager? That is a struggle we are only beginning to face, and it is a good news/bad news tale. The first big wave of involvement has passed. We can now look at what has washed up on the beaches. Who rode the wave well, and what can we learn from them? What organizations drowned in the sea of good intentions and what lessons do they give? We can learn from their successes and their failures. The next wave of higher involvement can be approached in a way that will call upon the resources and commitment of all staff.

The book is divided into three parts. Part One lays the foundation. It explores the reasons why organizations are searching for ways to involve people. It examines the practices that distinguish well-run organizations from those that have not found ways to build partnerships. It examines the reasons why employees like this trend. And finally it discusses the practices of some organizations that are using employee involvement strategies effectively.

Part Two invites you to focus on your work unit as you begin thinking about ways of applying the principles of employee involvement. It includes assessment of current attitudes and practices and discusses ways in which you can build a partnership between management and staff.

Part Three examines the daily leadership practices that nurture this process. This section discusses the ways to keep involvement high, day in and day out. It covers the new nine-to-five role of the supervisor and manager.

This book is not about manipulation or how to extract more from workers. It is based on the belief that you can form partnerships between management and staff to create workplaces that benefit individuals and organizations. It is too early to tell if this transformation in work will be a revolution or a failed rebellion. The answer lies in our willingness to learn from those who are proving that satisfaction and productivity are not only possible, but essential to success.

Acknowledgments

Hundreds of managers and staff helped me prepare this text. A special thanks goes to the people of the many organizations mentioned in the book who allowed me to spend time wandering about asking impertinent questions. To many others in corporations and government agencies who granted me telephone or breakfast interviews. To the men and women who attended the Center for Creative Leadership's Leadership Development Program at the University of Maryland, who know the problems of increasing involvement and partnership on the job and were willing to share their experience with me. To my clients who allowed me to test my ideas, prepare and revise some of the questionnaires you see in the text, and who never failed to detect fuzzy thinking or misguided idealism creeping through. To my colleagues in the organizational development profession who never fail to add to my thinking.

A special thanks to the readers of the first draft of this text: John Alaksa, Paul Bertolino, Carol Dell'Amore, Alan Gilburg, Ellen Harvey, Sally Johnstone, John Lathrop, Don Morrison, Carol Napolitano, Kathy Napolitano, Nora Redding, Ann Tarbell, Mark Walker, and Marc Young. They should take no blame for this book, but deserve much credit for its occasional glimmers of clarity.

Thanks to Karen Deans and her editing prowess for finding seemingly infinite ways of saying, "Didn't you really mean to say . . . ?," and for helping me stick to the point when I desperately wanted to ramble. To Willa Houtwed for proofreading and Sandra Palmer for book design of an earlier draft. And a special thanks to Productivity Press's acquisitions editor, Karen Jones, for making the process from manuscript to book so enjoyable.

Undoubtedly more names will come to me the moment this is set in type. I apologize in advance for those omissions.

I know of no safe depository of the ultimate powers of society but the people themselves; and if we think them not enlightened enough to exercise their control with a wholesome discretion, the remedy is not to take it from them, but to inform their discretion.

— Thomas Jefferson

Caught in the Middle

PART ONE

Understanding the Importance of High Involvement

1

Managing in a World without Rules

Unless American industry and other institutions begin to act on the need for quality in today's world, we are all going to be second-class citizens. It's no longer American industry versus American industry. It's American industry versus the world. Being involved with total quality is not just being nice, and it's not something that we like to do for the fun of it. It's essential to survival. This must be communicated more. And I don't think enough American corporations are paying attention.

— James R. Houghton
Chairman, Corning, Inc.

There is a quality rebellion going on; you may have heard about it. It seems that every magazine has published something about the Japanese threat. Every organization seems to have added terms such as "continuous improvement," "total quality management," and "customer service" to its list of operating tenets. Talk of quality is very popular.

The threat is real. The Japanese have beaten Western industry at its own game. Consumers, when offered quality, seem to prefer it, and companies that offer high-quality products and services have fared better. This news caused a massive shake-up in organizations, as everyone started scrambling to improve quality.

3

Some approached the challenge thoughtfully and changed the way they did business. Ford, for instance, began taking quality seriously. They called in W. Edwards Deming, the quality guru, and actually listened to him. They formed an innovative partnership with the United Auto Workers that gave more authority to hourly workers and increased both quality and job satisfaction. Because of poor quality, Harley-Davidson motorcycles were once rejected by so many consumers that the remaining Harley riders joked that instead of buying one Harley you should buy two, one to ride and one for parts. However, that has changed. Harley-Davidson is regaining market share rapidly, producing motorcycles with enviable quality standards. They did it through a combination of setting high standards of quality and creating ways of listening to the people who built the bikes.

Other organizations handled the challenge with the aplomb of the Keystone Kops responding to a bank robbery: by frantically flailing their arms, setting off in all directions, blaming everyone in sight, and making excuses. But unlike the silent film comedians, these organizations have not been able to save the day just in the nick of time. Those miracles happen only in the movies.

Recently, I worked with midlevel managers in a large bureaucracy who spoke derisively of the organization's push for total quality management. I was shocked. Isn't quality a worthy objective? Who could argue with so noble a concept as total quality management? I was told that TQM was merely the "flavor of the month": it required no changes in management practices, no examination of the relationships between suppliers and end users, no creation of quality standards, and no discussion of how to involve all staff in this new process. TQM was merely the "in" phrase to bandy about, proving that this organization was on the cutting edge. Last year senior management talked about "excellence," and before that it was "quality circles." The midlevel managers told me that they planned to lie low until this fad passed by.

Using the language of quality is simply not enough. Tom Peters is right when he says that we are in the "advanced lip service stage" of quality improvement. Ill-conceived improvement programs breed deserved skepticism and cause senior management to make excuses as to why these concepts can only work somewhere else, usually far across an ocean. I have been told that quality improvement and a key ingredient in getting there — true employee participation — cannot work in the federal government, in local government, in union/management environments, in large bureaucratic organizations, in the service sector, or in nonprofits. Everyone has a reason why it "won't work here."

Fortunately, not everyone is listening to this conventional wisdom. We can find examples of excellent cooperation in manufacturing, retail sales, telecommunications, school systems, and government agencies. Involvement works when people are willing to disregard the old rules and create new practices that are based on values as simple as openness, dignity, and trust.

We are entering the second phase of the quality uprising, and it has a chance of becoming a full-scale revolution. We now have evidence that quality improvement *can* work in America. We also know that organizations that treat people well and call on employees to use their brains do better in the marketplace. Robert Levering, in *A Great Place to Work*, reports on a number of studies that demonstrate this assertion. For instance, a Dean Witter Reynolds study found that if investors had bought stock in companies that treated their people well, they would have earned 17 percent more than if they had invested in a Standard & Poor's index fund. As S. Andrew Carson, author of one of the book's studies, said, "Overall, the study clearly showed that the more participatory the firm, the higher its level of financial and behavioral success."[2]

Companies that continue to play at the fringes of improvement cannot hope to compete. Philip Crosby estimates that many organizations spend from 20 to 35 percent of their operating budgets on the correction of mistakes.[3] Not only is that costly in dollars, making the company less competitive in price, but rework takes time, and that makes the company far less responsive to customer deadlines.

The pressures are mounting, and the leaders of organizations are clamoring to find out how the Japanese, the Xeroxes, the Marriotts, and the Cornings did it. Although they may sincerely want to rise above lip service, old ways of thinking may sabotage their good intentions.

The Dilemma of Change

In *Discovering the Future: the Business of Paradigms*, Joel Barker discusses the difficulty people have in shifting their thinking from one paradigm, or way of thinking, to another.[4] This inability to comprehend the need for new ways of approaching problems stands in the way of orderly change. Galileo was unsuccessful in getting the Roman Catholic church to see that Copernicus was correct in his hypothesis that the earth revolves around the sun and not the reverse. To accept Galileo's "proof" would be to seriously question the assumption that the earth was at the center of the universe. The church leaders could not see the same thing Galileo saw because their rules for understanding the universe did not permit such a vision.

Sticking to the old way of thinking is not obstinacy, but an inability to even see the possibility that something different could exist. When AT&T divested its many regional companies and was faced with competition not only from MCI but from its "Baby Bells," it acted for the most part as if nothing had happened. One marketing manager said her department was made up of two camps. The predivestiture camp wanted to approach marketing as it always had, and the postdivestiture group knew that it had to approach marketing quite differently if it wanted to compete. Intellectually, everyone knew that the company was no longer a monopoly, but in practice the old Ma Bell staff continued acting as if AT&T was everyone's favorite — and only — phone company.

It gets worse. Even when we recognize the need for change, we may not act effectively, because we don't know the rules of the new game. Since old rules seem better than no rules, we revert back to practices that worked in the past. Although corporate leaders may see the need to involve employees and improve quality, they may apply old management practices that cannot help them.

The head of one organization believes in all this talk about high participation and pushing control down to the lowest levels. He quotes the experts and sends his managers to training sessions that teach the current theories and practices. However, he is anything but an enlightened manager. He is autocratic, punishes any initiative that fails, and refuses to hear criticism. Ironically, his heart is in the right place, but his actions sabotage his good intentions. Old tried-and-true rules win out over the riskier ambiguity of a still-emerging way of operating.

One customer relations department wants to improve service to the public, but it evaluates its telephone reps on the speed with which they dispatch a complaint. To allow reps to spend the amount of time needed to do the job right would demand that managers trust employees to use good judgment. However, since computers can record the amount of time spent on a call, this measure — albeit the wrong measure — is used in a failed attempt to monitor "service." Even though managers know that the current way of measuring service is seriously flawed, they persist because they cannot find a way to measure good judgment. Their need to control wins out over the need to let employees do their jobs well.

Front-line supervisors face the same dilemma. Consider the supervisor who has enjoyed a successful career directing others. Once respected and rewarded by the organization for his take-charge approach, he now is told that he must be more "participative." Wanting to do a good job, he reverts to the only rules he knows — take charge and get the job done — and finds that the old rules fail him.

Where are the rules? Where are the textbooks that offer tidy step-by-step guidance? We are on the brink of an unprecedented revolution in quality and in how people are treated at work; therefore we cannot turn to history for guidance. That's both invigorating and frightening. Managers of one large government agency, seeing the need to change but skeptical that their agency could ever improve, beg for examples of excellent practice in other large, cumbersome agencies. They ask, "Show us how it's done. Prove to us that it works." There are no textbooks for them. If they are successful, the books will be written about them.

Emerging Rules

The fog is lifting. As we enter the second wave of quality improvement, we begin to see examples of excellent practice as well as many examples of failure. We can learn from the best and from those who dreamed of being best. Those who have gone before give us ideas, themes, perhaps even some rules for successful practice. We must examine both the best and the worst in order to begin patching together a working text that will guide us. We should begin by focusing on the twin themes of quality and partnership.

Quality. The best don't just talk about quality — they practice it. They believe that if they do it right the first time, ultimately they will save time, money, and migraines, and keep customers happy. In many ways, Ford exemplifies this almost religious concern for quality. They put Deming's principles into practice. They continually search for ways to improve the quality of their cars. The innovative Team Taurus, which invited design ideas from groups as diverse as hourly workers and the insurance industry and asked people on the front lines to carry out the first step in quality assurance, made Ford's commitment real in action. Workers on the assembly line know they are expected to produce high-quality parts the first time: if a part does not meet specifications, they must solve the problem or remove the part from the line. This commitment to quality is not evident in manufacturing facilities where quantity rules over quality. Nor does it exist in organizations where the standards of quality are unclear. Ford's motto — "Quality Is Job One" — states where its corporate values lie.

Continuous improvement. A hallmark of organizations that pay attention to quality and service is their constant search for ways to make things better. Deming says he is often asked, "How long will it take us to catch up with the Japanese?" His response: "Do you think the Japanese are standing still?" Insistence on constant improvement challenges the maxim, "If it ain't broke, don't fix it." As quality and service improve, expectations rise. The best know that the search for perfection is elusive, always just beyond reach.

The Department of Human Development in Fairfax County, Virginia, holds weekly Performance Improvement Team meetings in every operating unit in an effort to spot and correct problems that impede workflow. These sessions don't focus on scapegoats to blame; rather, they examine practices and procedures in an attempt to find better ways to provide service to the public.

Commitment to quality. Commitment to quality and service begins at the top. The trickle-down theory may not work in economics but it certainly works in changing attitudes and practices within organizations.

United Airlines decided to give all customer service agents more authority to make decisions. They wanted the agents to be able to solve customers' problems on the spot, eliminating the need to check with a supervisor. They developed a training program to get the word out. Instead of hiring a contractor to run the training or telling the training staff to conduct the sessions, senior managers went into the field to train the agents. Even though executives might not make the best instructors, the symbolism of this action far outweighed any flaws in their ability to run workshops. The fact that senior management themselves took the time to deliver the training said that they believed in this program.

Commitment to quality must be long-term. The best understand that significant improvement will not occur overnight, and that financial benefits will take even longer to materialize. They understand that their company will not feel the benefits of this healthy regimen in the short term, just as someone who gives up smoking, pork rinds, and a six-pack a day can't expect to regain good health overnight.

Customer-driven. These organizations measure just about everything by the customers' expectations. Managers and staff listen to the customers; they view complaints as an opportunity to learn something about their business. They know that the customer is their reason for being.

This focus extends to the internal customer as well. Every department, every person, begins looking at others in the company as customers. This leads to such unprecedented sights as engineers talking with their counterparts in manufacturing, and computer specialists listening to the fears and needs of their less computer-literate colleagues. Amazing.

Partnership. The other major theme is partnership. The best know that their people are their greatest resource, and they prove it by creating partnerships with them. This relationship, built on mutual self-interest, may take many forms. For example, a manufacturing company and a union developed a voluntary program in which workers were guaranteed employment for one year if they agreed to learn new skills and take more responsibility in the manufacture of a particular product. Most manufacturing companies simply lay people off when their production needs sag. And while other companies may look outside for talent, the Disney organization promotes from within. People there know that an entry-level job can be a stepping-stone to many other positions within the company. GE Mobile Communications shares its wins in the marketplace with hourly employees by linking bonuses to return on assets.

Organizations that build true partnerships among all staff find ways to share successes with the staff, encourage growth, and — more than simply making people feel as if they are part of the action — give them the authority and responsibility to make decisions and take actions that count.

The drive for quality and the commitment to partnership are two sides of the same coin; one will not exist without the other. This book focuses on the partnership side of that coin.

2

Traveling the Road to Hell

Whatever it is, I'm against it.
— Groucho Marx

The road to poor management is paved with good intentions. Building a partnership is difficult; few do it right. A partnership implies that we work with someone, rather than do unto them. This chapter focuses on the problems common to organizations whose managers are either neutral or actively hostile to the notion of giving more control to the people doing the work — often in spite of the good words coming from their lips.

Managers who believe in giving more authority to staff must understand the challenges they face in doing so. If your organization possesses the "Road to Hell" characteristics listed here, you must realize that you will have very little corporate support as you attempt to carry out the ideas in this book.

Risk Aversion

Risk-aversive organizations are so afraid of doing something wrong that they seldom do much right. One food products company was so afraid of putting a new dessert product on the market before thoroughly testing it that it watched competitors enter the market and create a firm foothold a year before its own product reached the stores.

CYA ("cover your anatomy") decisions often appear intelligent on the surface but mask a fundamental fear of doing the wrong thing. One large organization makes decisions by committee, assembling a team of people from all branches to ensure that all interests will be served in the project. The team often meets face-to-face to discuss proper procedures. Although one person is the committee chair, this person lacks authority to make decisions. Therefore, every draft must be approved by all members of the committee. When the project nears final draft stage, the committee members each send the draft out to their own staff members for comments and revisions. All votes are equal. In effect, the committee grows from a semicumbersome decision-making body to a committee six to ten times its original size.

> *It is human nature to think wisely and act foolishly.*
>
> — Anatole France

This may look like a sensible way of involving people — getting everyone in on the act — but it's not. It saps authority from the committee head. It slows decision making. It homogenizes creativity. The result is that the least offensive document is the one approved. If the person representing Unit A dislikes a portion of the text, it is deleted. The product is neither grand nor awful. It is simply the common product of bureaucrats making decisions.

Punishing the Offender

The fear of stiff punishment for taking risks is one reason that people avoid taking them. When someone is punished, the word spreads quickly, and soon few are willing to take that extra step to help a customer.

Once when friends and I were eating at a pizzeria, the service was slower than usual and the waitress offered us complimentary salads to curb our growing hunger and frustration. Another waitress complained that serving these salads would deplete the salad bar quicker and cause her more work. The manager sided with the complainer and reprimanded our waitress. I imagine she learned an important lesson for survival that day: never, under any circumstances, do anything extra for a customer.

Then there is the toast-at-noon faux pas. A customer asked the attendant at a cafeteria if he could have his tuna sandwich on toast. The employee complied, and his boss punished him by giving him a day without pay. Why? The cafeteria had a policy that toast could be served only at breakfast. (After all, if you let them have what they want at noon, who knows what they might ask for at dinner?)

Micromanagement

I distinguish micromanagement from the bureaucratic risk aversion mentioned above. The micromanaging leader trusts no one else to make the decision. Therefore, he or she personally makes all decisions.

For example, the founder of one small company takes pride in conducting all employment interviews and making all hiring decisions in spite of the fact that the company has grown quite large. On one hand, he appears to be a concerned boss who wants to maintain close contact with his staff by making certain he hires just the right people. This approach is right out of General Motors founder Alfred Sloan's book of management. On the other hand, it undermines the authority of all managers to hire the people they think are the best and tacitly suggests that they are incapable of making those weighty decisions.

In another example of micromanagement, one division director edits the reports of staff levels below her and insists that she approve all budget requests, no matter how small. Clearly, this woman needs a hobby.

Performance Appraisal System

Because performance review is a *system* with lots of columns and numbers and "management by objectives" minutiae, we assume it must be good. We do love our systems. Unfortunately, most performance appraisal systems are terrible. They work against the very partnership that organizations are trying to achieve.

Performance appraisal systems ultimately work against improvement. People fearful of the grade they are about to receive are not apt to talk candidly about performance issues. Since the systems single out individual achievement and failure, they identify heroes and scapegoats instead of examining the system people work in. They seldom examine the team's effectiveness, the relationship with customers and suppliers, or the boss's role in performance.

> *[The performance review] leaves people bitter, crushed, bruised, battered, desolate, despondent, dejected, feeling inferior, some even depressed, unfit for work for weeks after receipt of rating, unable to comprehend why they are inferior. It is unfair, as it ascribes to the people in a group differences that may be caused totally by the system they work in.*
>
> — W. Edwards Deming
> *Out of the Crisis*[1]

I recall a vice president of a large corporation once telling me how devastating it was to receive a "3" on a five-point scale. Despite the fact that his boss assured him that "3" really stood for "fully meets expectations," he felt that he had failed in some way.

Imagine the Juilliard String Quartet reviewing its performance at the end of the year. Would they demand that only one performer could possibly receive an A, two would earn C's, and one would be sent to a remedial music camp? Of course, that's absurd — they play as a team and succeed as a team.

Pack Rat Mentality

Pack rats drop old objects in favor of brighter, shinier, new ones. Like the organization mentioned in Chapter 1 that initiated total quality management as a "flavor of the month," many organizations grab hold of the latest theory, apply it superficially — often with great ceremony — then drop it when the next consultant on a book tour promises the Holy Grail.

Managers without Guidance

Managers are left to their own devices when attempting to define their new roles. Some succeed, some don't. Those who fail are pointed out as examples of the Peter Principle — the notion that people rise to their level of incompetence. Organizations create this phenomenon, then blame the individual.

Tradition

The Union Pacific Railroad was founded by retired Civil War generals who wanted to build a solid, no surprises organization. Until recently, that same management structure informed the actions of managers in that company. It was a rigid system that served well at a time when rapid westward expansion gave railroads all the business they could handle. It was not designed for a time when trucking and air freight could compete head-to-head with railroads. It was not designed to correct the market problems created when rail cargo traveled across the country at four miles per hour and a mere 60 percent of cargo arrived on time.

Being an employee in a hassling company is a lot like living at home after you grow up and having your parents decide all kinds of things for you.

— Philip Crosby
Quality without Tears[2]

The danger of tradition is that it can keep us from seeing the problem in front of us. In the 1970s, American auto makers were surprised when the public turned to foreign competition whose high-mileage cars offered relief from long gas lines. The threat of OPEC was not new: Detroit simply failed to consider the possibility that it needed to do business differently. Henry Ford once said that people could buy a Model T in any color they wished — as long as it was black. Some attitudes die hard.

Us versus Them

In some organizations the new partnership is only a veneer covering old beliefs. For example, a new employee involvement program may be used as a way to gain concessions or more work from employees without giving them any of the rewards.

This lack of regard for employees may work in the short run, but it will create a harsh backlash if it continues. Carnivals never stay in one town for long because cheap tricks and strange occurrences can't stand the close scrutiny of daily observation. Carnies know that they can't fool all of the people all of the time.

The traditional relationship between labor and management is so ingrained in our society that many organizations won't even consider the possibility of creating a partnership with their employees. Management, of course, should not take all of the blame. Some unions are trapped in old paradigms, failing to see the need for change. As a character in *Macbeth* describes the fighters in a battle, they are "two swimmers spent that do cling together and choke their art."

When a company traditionally lays off people at the first sign of a downturn or embraces two-week notices for plant closings, they can't expect inspired performance. Although they may argue the fiscal wisdom of giving short notice for plant closings, that strategy cannot build the kind of partnership that inspires people to travel the extra mile.

Depressed? Recognize people you know? This by no means definitive list may help you see the well-intentioned ways in which organizations hurt their chances for partnership. People in power must realize the impact these issues can have on the lives and work of the employees of the organization.

One theme underlies all the "Road to Hell" factors, and that is lack of trust. No participatory management or employee involvement process can succeed if management is unwilling to examine practices that undermine trust.

It is not just senior managers who travel the Road to Hell; occasionally people at your level do, too. In many of the following chapters, you will find sections that highlight the ways managers and supervisors unwittingly do things that work against their best intentions and lead them down the Road to Hell. Perhaps you'll be reminded of things you've done — and that's the point. Use this recognition to help you avoid repeating the same mistake.

3

Our Desire to Be Involved

I used to lie awake at night thinking about how they screwed me that day, then the next night I'd lie awake laughing as I thought about how I'd just screwed them.

— UAW member at Ford[1]

The new collaboration between labor and management in some auto plants is nothing short of astounding. Workers who did just enough to get by are now the first line of defense against poor workmanship. Managers who once shook their heads when they thought about the work force are now singing the praises of these same workers.

New United Motors Manufacturing Industry (NUMMI), a joint venture of General Motors and Toyota, boasts extraordinarily high productivity from its plant in Fremont, California. Customers like the vehicles produced at NUMMI, most workers enjoy their jobs, and the plant produces vehicles faster than most other GM plants. But there is more to the story.

Once the General Motors plant at Fremont was the joke of the auto industry — quality was awful, morale worse. Sometimes work had to wait until enough people appeared to begin operation. The plant was so unproductive that GM closed it rather than suffer more losses. Managers from the old days talk about the work force as a group of lazy people who just did not care about doing a decent job; nobody could manage these people.

When NUMMI opened, it hired back many of those "lazy incompetents" who are now making NUMMI so successful. Today the union workers at Fremont complete multiple tasks, stop the production line when they spot problems, and fix problems on the spot.

Conventional wisdom suggests that if people are unproductive, you should never give them more responsibility and control over their work. Yet, paradoxically, that is exactly what NUMMI did — and it paid off. It has to do with motivation.

Take care of your employees and they'll take care of your customers.

— J. Willard Marriott, Jr.

If you understand what motivates people on the job, you can begin to create an environment that inspires high commitment to quality and service.

What Motivates Us

Motivation is quite simple; most of us are motivated by similar things. When these things are present we work well, when they are absent, we complete our jobs with far less enthusiasm and commitment.

Before reading on, take a moment to consider the following. Think about a job you have held that met the following criteria:
- You enjoyed the work, and
- The quality of your work was very high.

Note the factors that made the work so satisfying.

_____

_____

_____

While it is true that people are motivated by different things —
some love to travel, others love to stay at home, for example —
there is a core group of needs or values that most of us find essential. If you want partnership, you must find ways to satisfy these
fundamental wishes. Compare your list to the following.

Meaning. We want to know that we count for something, that
we contribute in some way. We want our lives to have meaning. If
we are denied meaning at work, we look elsewhere and put our
energy into other areas of our lives. Work should not be the only
place where we find fulfillment, but it is the place where we spend
most of our waking hours. Eight hours a day of drone labor can
sap the spirit of most people.

Of course an organization cannot invent meaning or cram it
down employees' throats, but it can create a workplace where a
chance for fulfillment is possible. I have spoken to many people
who have said that work used to be "just a job," but since the initia-
tion of serious efforts on the part of their managers to involve
employees more fully, they have become proud of themselves and
their companies. They talk of caring about the quality of the work
and their coworkers.

Results. We like to finish what we start. We like the feeling of
accomplishment that comes from completing a task. Clear, measurable, and reachable goals stimulate us to take action and do the job.
When we cannot complete a job or have no way of measuring
progress, our commitment wanes.

Imagine you are a golfer. It's a beautiful Saturday morning,
and friends invite you to play at a new course. You arrive and find
an immaculate golf course. You place your ball on the first tee. As
you look down the fairway, you notice that there are no holes in the
green. Still, it's a beautiful day, you're here with friends, so you
decide to play. However, by about the fourth hole you are probably
beginning to think that this is about the dumbest way of spending
time you can imagine — and you're right. But add 18 tiny holes
every few hundred feet and you've got something. You've got a
game — and something to shoot for.

If you expect people to play enthusiastically you must provide tangible measures of accomplishment. They need a way of knowing how well they are doing.

Challenge. Most people want challenges and opportunities to grow. We want to know we are doing something better than it has been done before, that we are able to solve a particularly tough problem, or that we are learning something in order to do our job.

The golf course without holes offers no challenge for the player. It provides no way for the player to measure progress.

> *Any human anywhere will blossom into a hundred unexpected talents and capacities simply by being given the opportunity to do so.*
>
> — Doris Lessing

Although we love challenges, most of us do not desire impossible quests. Challenges must cause us to draw on our resources and make a dedicated effort to meet the goal, but we must always believe that the goal is reachable. If a goal is set too high, motivation diminishes. IBM management set sales quotas just high enough so that the sales force must work hard to meet them, but low enough so that persistent salespeople can reach them consistently. They understand that if they set quotas too high, only superstars like H. Ross Perot will meet the goals, and the rest of the sales force will feel like failures. And, as any salesperson will tell you, a salesperson who feels like a failure will be a failure.

Many find challenges in learning. Manufacturers are beginning to encourage hourly workers to learn a variety of skills, and paying them for using this new knowledge. The plant benefits from workers who can handle complex and varied tasks, and the individual benefits too. Instead of a mind-numbing shift of fitting ashtrays into dashboards, the worker is able to take a greater role in the production of the product.

Jazz trumpeter Clark Terry once said, "The only difference between a groove and a grave is the size of the rut."[2] Learning keeps the groove shallow. I recently spoke with a group of dentists regarding the high turnover among hygienists. It seemed that once the hygienists were terrific at cleaning teeth, there was little challenge left for them and they quit. Some dentists in the group had recognized this and expanded the role of the hygienist in the office. In one office, the hygienists were placed in charge of quality control and customer satisfaction. They determined ways to measure quality and service, as well as ways to keep quality high. In another office, the hygienists were responsible for all major purchasing. If the office needed a new piece of equipment, the hygienists determined the best equipment for the office and the dentist simply signed his or her name to the check.

Respect and recognition. People like to be treated with respect; that notion is so simple and yet so overlooked. You may recall the maxim, "Do unto others as you would have them do unto you." It's not bad advice, even if it didn't come from Harvard Business School.

Respect means treating people with the same dignity that you expect to be treated with. Years ago, two of my coworkers and I took a business trip across the country with the head of the company. She flew first class; we didn't. On arrival, a colleague met us and asked about the trip. Our boss said, "My trip was fine, but, of course, I don't know what it was like back there in steerage."

On the other hand, when NUMMI had a cutback on production, they did something unusual for a GM plant — they kept the people on. They found work for them. The message was clear: You are the cause of our success and we will stick with you during rough times. Too often recognition for a job well done goes only to the executives on Mount Olympus.

Respect is bedrock. You owe people the courtesy of showing respect for them. Recognition, on the other hand, is something people must earn. Having earned something, people naturally like to be recognized for their accomplishments. Recognition can take many forms, from awards at a rubber-chicken banquet to a bonus to a simple "thank you."

Often we forget to tell those who do good work exactly what we think. Eddie Murray, one of the all-time great hitters for the Baltimore Orioles, was a catalyst for his teammates. When he was hitting well, his performance seemed to inspire others. When asked if that was true, he replied that he had no way of knowing, since he was always at the plate whenever they felt inspired.

Control. We all like to feel we are in control. Consequently, we want to have control over the work we do. That doesn't mean that a machinist wants to control marketing decisions for the company; rather, that she simply wants to know that she has the power to make decisions regarding her work.

Affiliation. People refer to affiliation as the desire to work on a good team or with good people. Wanting to work with others does not necessarily implicate a desire to be joined at the hip to the other members of the team, or a need to sit in meetings all day, but it does represent a wish to be part of a group where one's work stimulates the thinking of others and synergy develops; where victories and defeats are shared; and where there is a feeling that one is part of a larger group working toward a common end.

These six themes do not address all the factors that motivate us, but they are a good start. You need only ask those who work in the best organizations, "What do you like about it?" and you will hear these terms and their synonyms used repeatedly. Ask people in the hellish organizations, "Why do you dislike it here?" and you will hear the antonyms of this list.

The Road To Hell and the False X

Douglas McGregor suggested that managers view the world in one of two ways — as a Theory X world or a Theory Y world.[3] If we see the world as Theory X, we assume that people are lazy and would rather goof off than apply themselves to any serious endeavor. If our view of the world is Theory Y, we assume that those people out there are as excited about work as we are. Work is

[Q] *Did the line people, the production people, resist being responsible for their own technology?*

[A] *Not at all. We've always done things that way. The line is responsible for safety; the line is responsible for training; the line is responsible for hiring. Well, we do have a couple of trainers but only because they have very specific things to do in electronics. We have no staff group for training, though. We don't delegate that kind of thing.**

— Gordon E. Forward
Chairman, Chaparral Steel[4]

viewed as being as natural as play, and it is believed to be the manager's job to create an environment in which hard-working people (like you and me) can flourish.

McGregor said that, in the past, many organizations treated people as if Theory X were true. Today, most managers have been indoctrinated with the serum of Peters and Waterman and know enough not to express viewpoints that come from the canon of Theory X. However, that doesn't stop managers from actually using Theory X practices.

Most managers believe in the principles of motivation listed above, but unwittingly create practices that are pure Theory X. The result is that perfectly fine employees respond exactly as they are treated, and for all the world they look like the embodiment of Theory X. People lower themselves to our expectations, so that we have successfully created a work force of False X's.

One research organization found that some employees were abusing flextime. Their solution to this problem: require all staff to

---

* Reprinted by permission of *Harvard Business Review*. An excerpt from "Wide-open management at Chapparal Steel," Gordon E. Forward, interviewed by Alan M. Kantrow (May/June 1986). Copyright © 1989 by the President and Fellows of Harvard College; all rights reserved.

punch in and out on time clocks. By doing so, management sent a stunning message to these highly educated professionals — that they could not be trusted to put in a fair day's work. The impact was devastating. Productivity plummeted and so did morale.

A manager in a federal agency (and I swear I'm not making this up) allowed employees five minutes to use the rest room when the call came during work rather than break time. If a miscreant took more than the allotted time, this diligent civil servant went in after them. He walked into the men's and the women's rooms with equal resolve — the very model of equality in action.

It doesn't take much to see the folly in these decisions, but managers make similar, albeit quieter, mistakes in judgment every day — for example, when an employee must have a decision approved by six people. When the manager checks and double-checks every bit of correspondence. When redundancy is built in to cover every conceivable "just in case" scenario. Each of these actions tells the employee that he or she is not capable of using good judgment. If the explicit message to us is that we can't be trusted to go to the toilet unattended, then the implicit message is that we can't be trusted to do anything substantive without a guardian.

Too much oversight, too much protection against contingencies, creates a work force that resembles a cast party for *The Night of the Living Dead*. We create zombies. After creating them, we look at them and shrug our shoulders. After all, who could be expected to manage workers like these?

What About the Real X's?

> *The best don't need rules and the worst won't be helped by them.*
>
> — Voltaire

While it is true that there are a few X's out there, most people are motivated by precisely the things that motivate you. The DNA structure of executives and managers is no different than the DNA pattern of hourly workers. Doesn't it make sense to play the odds and create a work environment that encourages the 95 percent who do want to face challenges, rather than create a prison for the few who don't want to work?

Summary

Tom Peters said, "There is no limit to what the average person can accomplish if thoroughly involved."[5] To increase the commitment to quality and service, you must find ways to build on your own natural desires and wishes as well as on those of the people who report to you. People want to do good work. The factors behind motivation — meaning, results, challenge, respect and recognition, control, and affiliation — are more than just nice ways to treat people. They are essential ingredients in creating the level of commitment you need in order to succeed.

Although it helps if the organization encourages treating people with dignity and showing appreciation for the needs of individuals, there is absolutely no reason why line managers cannot tend to these values without help from above. In the worst of organizations, there are people who treat others well — who do their best to live by the values discussed in this chapter. The values of motivation provide the foundation for all management practices described in the remaining chapters.

4

Considering the Options

There are no constraints put on your work; consequently, there is no excuse for doing anything less than excellent work.
— Producer with the Film Board of Canada

Some of you are embarking on an employee involvement process that was selected for you. Perhaps your company has decreed that self-managed teams will be the new way branch offices operate. Others of you may be searching for a way to increase involvement within your own unit. In either case, it's important to know the range of options others have tried.

This chapter merely gives you a lay of the land. Please don't pick an approach as if it were a prepackaged product you could purchase off a shelf with no assembly required. Every effort at involvement that I have seen succeed has been created or adapted especially to the unique characteristics of the organization. Think of the processes described here as catalysts for thinking about what might work in your organization.

Suggestion Systems

Suggestion systems offer structured ways to get lots of ideas for improvement on issues as diverse as quality improvement, morale, safety, cost savings, and ease of work. They are perhaps the oldest form of participative involvement. For instance, in 1721,

> a small box called the *meyasubako* was placed at the Takinoguchi entrance to Edo Castle by the order of Yoshimune Tokugawa, the eighth shogun. All citizens, regardless of their social standing, were allowed to drop written suggestions, requests, and complaints into the box. The *meyasubako* was the shogun's way of finding out how people felt about his policies and what people were thinking in general. Good suggestions were rewarded, and a man . . . wrote a suggestion that led to the opening of a health-care facility for the poor.[1]

Typically, suggestion systems are open to all employees, although many of the existing programs focus heavily on the hourly work force. Employees are encouraged to make suggestions, usually on a simple form, explaining the nature of the problem and what they propose to do to solve it. The emphasis is on day-to-day improvements that the employee can implement — ideas that make his or her work easier or more efficient, or that serve the customer more effectively. Often, proposed solutions can be implemented by the employees themselves; for example, reorganizing a work station or using a machine in a slightly different manner. Suggestion programs sometimes encourage employees to recommend procedures that could change the organization of an entire system. Note that suggestions are not gripes, but statements of problems and proposed solutions.

A team at the work-unit level evaluates ideas, approves those that have merit, and sends rejected ideas back with an explanation. Usually the system allows an appeal of sorts, so that if an employee feels strongly about the proposal, he or she can try again. Proposed solutions that would cost a significant amount or could have an impact on other parts of the organization are sent to a higher evaluation team for consideration.

Suggestion systems usually work best when they are part of an integrated approach to improving quality, service, or efficiency. Say an organization announces that waste reduction is a top priority over the coming months; suggestions can then be targeted toward achieving this corporate objective. The system works best when supervisors and managers take an active role in encouraging ideas from workers, discussing ways to improve on the ideas and helping get the suggestions implemented.

Japanese organizations often institute suggestion systems in three stages. Stage One encourages quantity — anything goes. This gets people thinking and lets people address nagging pet peeves as a way of testing the system. Placing too many restrictions on what is allowable at this stage may inhibit participation. Stage Two teaches people how to analyze problems and create workable solutions. This begins to put more power into the hands of the people closest to the problems. Stage Three focuses on economic impact; however, it may take years to reach this last stage.[2] This system is a far cry from the Western penchant for immediate bottom-line results.

Variations. Consider these suggestions for getting employee ideas.

The suggestion box. The dusty old suggestion box is taking on a new look. The Scottsdale, Arizona, city government uses a "This Seems Dumb to Me" suggestion box system. Anyone can make a suggestion anonymously and know that the suggestion will be considered seriously. There's nothing wrong with this idea; the name itself is inspired. It allows anyone to make comments. It works for the city, and results in improvements.

Some would say that suggestion boxes are one stop on the continuum of employee involvement, albeit the lowest stop on the scale. However, as helpful as they may be, they cannot be considered the type of employee involvement that builds partnership. Although they give people a voice, they do not touch the deeper aspects of self that mark true involvement. Suggestion boxes put the power into the hands of those who own the key. The challenge of true involvement is finding ways to give everyone a key to the box.

Ad hoc groups. A department in a publishing company occasionally convenes meetings that include customer service representatives and some managers. There is no formal structure to these meetings. They are led by the simple and direct question, "What drives you crazy?"

In one meeting, managers learned that when customers called complaining that they had paid their bill and had a canceled check to prove it, policy dictated that the reps ask them to photocopy the check — front and back — and mail it in. This made customers angry and embarrassed staff. Often they would invent new procedures rather than ask customers to mail in photocopies.

Managers asked what information the reps needed to verify payment. Since all they needed was the check number and the name of the bank, there really was no need to see the check. Managers changed the policy.

These ad hoc meetings are effective. As Philip Crosby would say, they help "de-hassle" the workplace, and they are easy to convene with no change in policy or management structure. These meetings succeed when managers willingly listen to the "what drives you crazy" complaints, and then take action.

Ad hoc meetings are a good start, but problems should be spotted when they occur and solved quickly. The informal approach may limit good and time-sensitive ideas simply because no one thinks to convene a meeting.

Advantages. Suggestion systems often spark great interest. People who have felt anonymous suddenly can give voice to ideas that have remained dormant for years. They provide easy, no-risk ways of giving ideas to management.

The Winshare process at GE Mobile Communications reported that suggestions from the factory floor saved the company $9 million in 1989. In addition, many other small ideas were implemented — things that made work easier or removed petty hassles. These weren't measured for cost savings, but did improve the quality of life on the floor.

One measure of the success of suggestion systems is the number of people getting involved by submitting ideas. The Total Employee Involvement (TEI) Newsletter suggests that such programs need not reach 100 percent involvement to be effective.[3] At just 25 to 30 percent, the process can hit a critical mass, becoming a vehicle for employee involvement and not just another idea dreamed up by management. Some organizations report reduced absenteeism, fewer grievances, and significant quality improvements. Not bad.

Limitations. Suggestion systems do not alter the structure of the workplace and so may be limited to improvements that can be made within existing boundaries and relationships. If the company is on a good course, this may not be much of a limitation. However, in an organization that lacks clear direction, suggestions cannot be evaluated against a standard, since individuals have no way of knowing the priorities. In other words, lots of resources can be expended solving insignificant problems.

Quality Circles

The quality circle is one of the most popular involvement processes in the United States, and for good reason. Its problem solving methods are simple, effective, and easily learned. And the process can be implemented with no change in management structure. It's no wonder that the methods of the circle are used in all manner of involvement processes, including suggestion systems.

Typically, a circle made up of volunteers meets once a week to examine quality issues and make recommendations for improvement. Teams receive training in group process, problem analysis, and decision making, and sometimes in statistical process control. Facilitators run the meetings according to a prescribed format. Often these facilitators receive special training in group dynamics to assist them in keeping meetings productive.

When circles are used throughout the organization, a steering committee oversees their work. This committee may provide training, suggest expenditure of funds, coordinate work among circles, and champion circle ideas that cut across organizational lines.

Variations. In many organizations, the quality circle structure and methods have been used to tackle other issues such as safety or morale. The U.S. Postal Service uses circles they call work teams, but they broaden the scope to include almost anything the teams consider important. For instance, one group had doors replaced to cut down on vandalism, and a higher fence built to deter beer-bottle athletes from lobbing empties over onto parked vehicles.

Other organizations use the methods of the circle in hit teams or ad hoc problem-solving committees formed to address a single issue.

Advantages. Circles have a long history; there is much to be learned from their successes and their failures. More has been written about the circle than about any other form of employee involvement, so it is easy to find good training in its methods. The Association for Quality and Participation, a professional organization devoted to the issue of high involvement, was originally named the International Association for Quality Circles, and many of those who attend AQP conventions are members of circles or work teams.

Where circles work, enthusiasm is high. Teams take pride in talking about the money saved, increased quality, and new, improved relationships between management and staff.

Limitations. The circle can simply run out of things to do. This occurs most often when the charge to the circle is limited to making small and inexpensive changes. Some groups have felt that once they have fixed up the bathrooms, settled on which radio station to play in the unit, and obtained a bulletin board, their work is finished. Sometimes they are right.

The built-in limitation of the circle is that a small group meets for just one hour a week. This leaves 39 hours and countless other people who may not be involved. A circle may have little impact on how people work together most of the time. The one-hour-a-week nod to involvement may be similar to that of my friends in high school who attended church services on Saturday evening to get them out of the way, so that they could have the rest of the weekend free to do whatever they wanted.

The Postal Service has recognized the limitations of the circle and is encouraging postal facilities to push involvement further. They see the circle as a well-structured way in which to begin the involvement process, and once established, to be discarded in favor of higher forms of involvement.

Self-managed Teams

The self-managed team is the most sophisticated employee involvement process in common practice. A self-managed team is aptly named. It may set priorities and activities and manage its own time. It may do its own hiring and develop job descriptions for team members. On some teams, members give each other performance evaluations.

Although the team may have a single manager who is the team leader, in many respects it is a confederation of equals. Leadership is assigned based on projects rather than rank. Today a general may work for a captain, tomorrow for a lieutenant, and the next day may find himself or herself in charge. Leadership is a functional responsibility.

More than any of the other approaches, the self-managed team demands the highest degree of commitment to the values of employee involvement. The self-managed team concept doesn't just thrive on the notion that people will rise to challenges — it requires this belief. In an environment in which people are expected to spot their own errors and take corrective actions with no one hovering above to guide and prod, trust is essential.

The trend seems to be toward greater use of these teams. While the quality circle concept is most popular in production facilities, the self-managed team cuts across organizational types freely. Unlike the quality circle, no single approach captures the spirit or design of the self-managed team. At Milliken, a manufacturer of textiles, entire shifts operate without managers present. At branches of the Capitol Holding Company, self-directed teams create their own design for work in a continual effort to better serve customers.

Advantages. The self-directed team has the potential to meet the values that motivate us at work — meaning, results, challenges, respect, and control. Employees are treated like thinking beings and asked to create a work structure and way of operating that fits their unique environment.

More than the other approaches described above, the self-directed team can transform the role of manager into that of a leader among equals. Freed from the power and need to use coercion as a management tool (e.g., elimination of performance appraisals in some enlightened organizations), managers find that the quality of the relationship improves. They discover that their role in what gets done is no more or less significant than that of other members of the team.

Limitations. The trend toward self-directed teams, if it continues, signals a further reduction in first-level supervision and management. As teams take over many of the tasks heretofore assigned to managers, many positions, particularly those limited to monitoring and policing work closely, will be eliminated. Organizations are finding that they don't need the "cop on the corner" to keep order.

But all is not lost. There is, and probably will always be, a need for those who can lead the work of teams and individuals. Even at Milliken, managers coordinate work between shifts and perform higher level tasks than would be appropriate for manufacturing teams. At Capitol Holding, managers still hire, promote, and perform many of the functions we expect from managers, while the team is responsible for many decisions regarding structure and approach. Supervisors and managers who are willing to see the new paradigm, and who recognize that it may require a set of very foreign and seemingly "soft" skills, should be in a far better position to survive and flourish during the organization's shift to self-managed teams.

Think Expansively

It may be tempting to limit your thinking to the three most well-known approaches — suggestion systems, quality circles, and self-directed teams — because of their popularity. While one of these may be perfect for you, I encourage you to think expansively before settling on a particular approach.

High involvement rests on a foundation of strong shared values, not on specific techniques. The motivation factors described in Chapter 3 — meaning, results, growth, respect and recognition, control, and affiliation — are essential themes in any successful process. Without these values, any of the approaches listed above would be "just another program," doomed to failure. Suggestion systems will fail if people believe the organization doesn't care about them. Quality circles will stagnate if employees believe they are nothing more than management's inexpensive and visible way of pretending it cares about people. Self-directed teams will die if people see them as simply a way to reduce the work force.

The possibilities for high involvement seem to have no bounds; they are limited only to the resourcefulness of the people involved. Just when it appears that self-directed teams are the last word in involvement, along comes Semco, a Brazilian manufacturing company that gives management and union personnel equal votes in critical decisions and allows people to set their own salaries.

The Dana Corporation keeps its units small, believing that people do best when they can rub shoulders with their colleagues in other departments. When things get too big and bureaucratic, they break up into smaller operating units.

One manager in a large bureaucracy lives these values by making staff meetings, phone conversations, and "management by wandering around" opportunities for meaningful exchanges about ideas and methods. She listens, considers, debates, and, most of all, respects the men and women who report to her. Her staff would say that they work with her, rather than for her. Although this manager uses none of the formal techniques of involvement, her office is a model of high commitment and equally high quality.

The idea of working "with," rather than "for," changes the way we view this relationship. Max DePree, chairman of the Herman Miller Company, suggests that employees today are essentially volunteers.[4] When they don't like what's going on, they can leave, or, in the more elegant words of Johnny Paycheck, tell their employers to "take this job and shove it."

The employee-manager relationship changes when we consider it to be a voluntary arrangement. The implicit power to coerce is removed and we begin to see new possibilities for relationships built on mutual interests. While it is true that some organizations still thrive on nineteenth-century sweatshop tactics, their days may be numbered, as their more enlightened competitors learn that working in partnership with "volunteers" gives them the strong value-added benefit of high commitment.

Options and the Road to Hell

The following are some traps to avoid when choosing an approach for your own involvement effort.

The quick fix. Begin quality circles on Monday and see an increase in profits by Friday. No one seriously believes that, but our practices often make it appear as if this myth were true. Quick fixes breed only more quick fixes. Real change takes time.

Too much too soon. These processes often fail when they are rolled out with great fanfare and ceremony, only to die because no one was truly committed to the change. This breeds well-deserved skepticism.

The showcase. Sometimes involvement programs are used as a convenient way to demonstrate that the organization believes in people, when the opposite is true. People will see through the showcase.

Buying a package. Beware of consultants bearing gifts. Involvement is more than a packaged program; it is a new way of treating people. No prepackaged program will work without serious examination and willingness to adapt it to the culture and demands of the particular organization.

First aid when surgery is needed. A slight nod toward involvement — say, inviting people once a year to tell you what's on their minds — cannot be expected to change the problems of low morale or poor quality.

When the going gets tough, retreat. One manufacturing company, after investing a considerable amount in improving the partnership between management and craft workers, eliminated the involvement process when the budget got tight. If we believe that higher involvement will improve quality and eventually earnings, then eliminating the process during hard times makes no more sense than trying to save money by purchasing lower quality materials.

The issue facing you is not so much which technique to apply, but how to foster the values that build the foundation for involvement. The deeper and more solid the foundation, the higher the structure you can build. No option offers a panacea. They all require commitment, dedication to learning and applying new skills, and hard work. Implementation will not be perfect. Others will err, and perhaps you will, too. Expect problems and challenges, but use the values as a touchstone as you form partnerships with staff.

PART TWO

Getting Started

5

Assessing Yourself

It is in the trifles, and when a man is off his guard, that he best shows his character.

— Arthur Schopenhauer

Before you announce your grand plan to change the workplace, take a few moments for a close look at yourself. Are you ready for all this? If you are not — if you lack enthusiasm or the requisite leadership skills — the chances of making involvement work are dismal.

The following informal assessment should help you determine your readiness to proceed.*

Self-Assessment: Am I Ready?

Score your reaction to the following statements, from 1 = you've got to be kidding, to 7 = I couldn't agree more.

---

*This and the other self-diagnostic tools in the book are reprinted in Appendix B for easy reference and reproduction.

Commitment

I believe that pushing maximum control down to the people closest to the product or customer is a wise move. I believe that this will increase the commitment to quality and service among staff and will therefore increase the quality of the work we do.

1_____2_____3_____4_____5_____6_____7

Work Process Skills

I have the skills needed to analyze work flow and statistical quality control, and know how to use problem analysis and problem-solving techniques, such as constructing Pareto charts.

1_____2_____3_____4_____5_____6_____7

Knowledge of Organization

I have a thorough understanding of the reasons why employee involvement is important to our organization and how my unit fits into the move toward higher quality and service.

1_____2_____3_____4_____5_____6_____7

Employee Involvement Orientation

I understand how the various involvement options can be applied and have a good understanding of what can work and what will fail in my type of organization.

1_____2_____3_____4_____5_____6_____7

Leadership Skills

These are the leadership skills you should use to build a partnership with your staff. Each skill is discussed at length in the chapters of Part Three.

1. Setting Direction
   A. How well do I state and clarify vision, goals, and objectives?

   ```
   1_____2_____3_____4_____5_____6_____7
   Poorly                               Very Well
   ```

   B. How well do I lead by example? Do my actions demonstrate a commitment to employee involvement?

   ```
   1_____2_____3_____4_____5_____6_____7
   Poorly                               Very Well
   ```

2. Keeping Others Informed
   A. How well do I give helpful and timely feedback regarding performance?

   ```
   1_____2_____3_____4_____5_____6_____7
   Poorly                               Very Well
   ```

   B. How well do I keep others informed regarding changes in the business or the work of other units?

   ```
   1_____2_____3_____4_____5_____6_____7
   Poorly                               Very Well
   ```

3. Initiative
   A. How well do I encourage people to take risks?

   ```
   1_____2_____3_____4_____5_____6_____7
   Poorly                               Very Well
   ```

B. How well do I use failed risks as learning opportunities (or do I punish the risk-taker)?

1_____2_____3_____4_____5_____6_____7
Poorly   Very Well

4. Support
How well do I give people support and encouragement?

1_____2_____3_____4_____5_____6_____7
Poorly   Very Well

5. Development
A. How well do I provide the help people need to develop skills to do their jobs?

1_____2_____3_____4_____5_____6_____7
Poorly   Very Well

B. How well do I provide support for people's career development?

1_____2_____3_____4_____5_____6_____7
Poorly   Very Well

6. Coordinating Effort
A. How well do I coordinate work within this work unit?

1_____2_____3_____4_____5_____6_____7
Poorly   Very Well

B. How well do I coordinate work between this unit and our suppliers and customers?

1_____2_____3_____4_____5_____6_____7
Poorly   Very Well

7. Building a Team
   How well do I encourage the development of a healthy work team?

   1_____2_____3_____4_____5_____6_____7
   Poorly   Very Well

8. Keeping Yourself Informed
   How well do I encourage and accept criticism from others?

   1_____2_____3_____4_____5_____6_____7
   Poorly   Very Well

Interpretation

Commitment

1 to 3 points. Introducing involvement processes may be very difficult for you. Determine whether your low score reflects a distrust in the people currently assigned to you or a basic distrust of this process.

If you are concerned that your staff is not up to this challenge, remember that in many places, managers who swore they were working with turned-off Theory X people before introducing these processes now enjoy an increased partnership and commitment to quality and service.

Identify what it will take for you to increase your commitment to this process. Talk with others who have made it work. Ask them how they got over the initial fear and resistance to change. Take heart: others have been skeptical, too.

Finally, a warning: look to the future. Increasing the partnership between management and staff is gaining in popularity. If that's true in your organization, consider the implications for managers who don't embrace this concept.

4 to 5 points. You may be taking a "wait-and-see" attitude. But if you wait, what you'll see is that nothing will change. Success demands your leadership. Your staff can't lead you.

Learn more about the process and how it has worked. Visit places where it has worked and ask managers tough questions: Do they like the new arrangement? What challenges do they face? Would they go back to the old way if they could?

Determine what it will take for you to increase your commitment to this process.

6 to 7 points. You probably are wondering why the organization waited so long to begin this process. For years you've known it would work.

Work Process Skills

Note: The tools such as statistical process control may not be appropriate to your business. If not, a low score is nothing to worry about. However, problem analysis and decision-making tools can work quite effectively in most settings.

1 to 3 points. If you need these skills in your organization, consider begging the human resources or quality assurance department to offer this training.

4 to 5 points. A refresher course might be in order.

6 to 7 points. Seems as if you are in good shape.

Knowledge of Organization

1 to 5 points. Determine where you must go to get answers to your questions. Some questions you might consider asking:

- Does corporate headquarters have a plan for increasing involvement?

- Does the organization have a set of values or a vision that is guiding its action?
- Who is driving this process? (The CEO? No one?)
- What support and resources can I expect from the organization?
- Have other units within the organization started involvement processes? Have they been successful?

6 to 7 points. You are probably ready to get started.

Employee Involvement Orientation

1 to 5 points. You need more information. Fortunately, many options are available to you. Consider the following:

- Appendix A lists many resources — books, tapes, case studies — that describe employee involvement as well as quality and service improvement issues.
- Other units within your organization may have already struggled with these same issues. Call or visit them and pump them for information — what works, what doesn't, what they would do differently if they could.
- Occasionally, the human resources department will have good information on ways of implementing employee involvement processes.

6 to 7 points. Good luck. Just remember, what worked on Broadway may bomb in Peoria. An involvement process that worked at a General Electric plant cannot be dropped into J.C. Penney and be expected to work. Keep your mind and your options open.

Leadership Skills

Consider each score individually. Don't average the scores. For instance, if you gave yourself a 6 on seven categories and a 1 on a single category, don't assume that you earned a grade of 5.4. Consider the low score separately — it has something to tell you.

1 to 5 points. Effective use of these skills can have a significantly positive impact on the implementation of the involvement process. Examine each category. Take low to mid-range scores seriously. Skip ahead to Part III and read the chapters that discuss your lower scores, and then develop a plan to improve these skills.

6 to 7 points. Feeling smug? Consider giving the questionnaire in Chapter 17 to your staff to see if they agree with your high score.

Self-Assessment and the Road to Hell

Here are some points to watch for in assessing your situation.

Yeah, yeah, yeah. Yes, you've heard all this touchy-feely stuff before, and you frankly don't have time for it. The tendency may be to get on with it — "give me a program I can implement and get it over with." Slow down. Build a foundation before moving ahead.

The problem's over there. It's those other people who will ruin this effort — senior management, the union, the folks down the hall. Once they get in line, just watch me shine.

Look carefully at yourself before proceeding — increasing involvement could be a wonderful opportunity for you, or it could be pure, screaming hell. Before you proceed, learn all you can about the issues of involvement and participation, quality and service improvement — and yourself. Do whatever it takes to make sure you are ready for this change before moving ahead.

6

Creating a Partnership

Rules
1. The boss is always right.
2. When the boss is wrong, refer to Rule 1.

— Paul Dickson[1]

Efforts to give more authority to staff fail when leaders attempt to make changes unilaterally or workers perceive that the changes will benefit only management or stockholders. The history of labor-management relations in this country offers good counsel for all managers wishing to initiate changes.

After a century of struggle between labor and management, it should not surprise anyone that each side views the other with suspicion and distrust. Any change by management may be seen as an attempt to harm labor — reduce jobs, lower wages, seek benefits concessions, or bust the union. If management wants to create self-directed teams or give more authority to individuals, it must understand this long-standing antipathy toward management actions.

Labor's reaction to self-directed teams and other forms of pushing control down the organization is mixed. Some unions fight efforts to make these changes. One paper company suffered a six-month strike over the issue of self-directed teams. Other unions see this movement as the only way American industry can stay competitive and keep jobs for members. Some take a "wait-and-see" attitude.

Organized labor has a voice, so it is easier for us to hear their fears and warnings. But employees who lack a unified voice have the same fears and questions as their unionized counterparts.

Fear and distrust will not be overcome easily. Workers who feel they have been wronged in the past will approach change warily. Managers who feel workers are lazy are likely to initiate changes with skepticism. Employees who know about the nature of labor-management relations of a generation ago only through legend and rumor will hold onto that view as if it happened to them last week.

Like it or not, you may be the embodiment of the organization to your staff. If your organization uses boneheaded performance review procedures, fires people easily, or punishes initiative, you may be seen as the chief bonehead. You may need to prove to your staff that you can be trusted in spite of what the organization might have done in the past.

Trust is elusive — it is difficult to build and easy to destroy. Others have learned that trust cannot be earned by words alone. Merely saying "I am not a crook" does not offer the proof people need.

Building the Partnership

Trust first. Trust your staff to do what is best for the organization and themselves. Assume that people will act responsibly. Ask their opinions and give them authority, working in partnership with them. If they abuse your trust, you can always retreat. But you are not likely to make progress if you wait cautiously for them to prove they are worthy of your trust.

When trust must be earned — when people must jump a long course of hurdles before you award them a medal for trustworthiness — people feel the implied distrust and give less than their best efforts.

Assume the transition will be difficult. Assume the employees will be fearful and wary of these changes by management. Take every precaution to ensure that the employees see management actions as trustworthy and aboveboard. The only way you can increase commitment is to build a partnership.

You must continually put yourself in their shoes. Constantly ask: How are they likely to respond to this? What assurances would I want if I were in their position?

Play your cards face up. When the chance of confusion and misinterpretation is high, you must always be open. Don't play your cards close to the vest. You are playing on the same side of the table with the employees — you *must* show your hand. This includes telling people why you want to make these changes and the potential consequences. It may involve opening the company's books. Keep people informed of decisions and potential changes in the works.

One CEO of a manufacturing company prepared a videotape that explained the reasons for the shift to self-directed teams, the consequences if the company failed to regain its competitive position, and his expectations for implementation. Results of a study of the competitive environment were made available to all personnel, both management and labor. The moment a rumor began circulating, managers responded directly, either confirming the truth of the gossip or explaining what really was going on.

Throughout the long and often arduous process of building commitment to a joint plan between management and labor, managers kept the books open and answered every question. Finally, after six months of hard work, the organization had its plan for quality improvement and employee participation. It was a plan that had the full consent of all interested parties — corporate headquarters, plant management, and the six unions!

Form the partnership early. Bring employees into the planning process as soon as you are committed to going ahead. Don't wait. People are used to parental management approaches in which management makes all the decisions — and they hate it. These are the people who will have to give 100 percent effort for the project to succeed. They know their jobs, they know the problems involved — use their valuable knowledge.

Consider creating a steering committee to help you devise and implement the changes. The committee should have power to make decisions and be a significant voice in the process.

If you are the manager of a group of five people, you don't need a committee. Simply invite everyone to talk with you about the involvement process. If you manage a larger and broader group, you should carefully consider whom to invite. The next section may help you make that decision.

Include all interested parties. Make certain that all constituencies are included in the process. If you are a high school principal, you might include some teachers, secretaries, parents, custodians, and students. An accounting office might include significant internal customers, senior management, clerical staff, and so forth.

Invite some people who have strong points of view and who may disagree with your views. As hard as this may be, it is better to hear their arguments now than have them sabotage the process later. Building bridges increases commitment to the process.

Include people who are interested in seeing change occur. They could be active champions of the process.

The committee should be large enough to include all interests and small enough to allow the group to work effectively as a planning team. If you manage a very large operation — for example, if you are in charge of product development and have four or five diverse branches reporting to you — consider ways that the core steering committee can encourage questions and suggestions from the entire staff throughout the planning process.

Peter Block, in *The Empowered Manager*, suggests that these "stakeholders" be considered on two dimensions, trust and agreement.[2] Those who agree with us and with whom we have a high level of mutual trust might be considered allies. These people are easy to work with. We need not be on guard or worry about using the right words; they are on our side.

Opponents are people with whom we enjoy high trust, but who may disagree on direction. A manager in a government agency feels that the good relationship with her boss is due in large part to

> *For more than 30 years, [Delta] has let nonunion workers select lead mechanics and quality control supervisors. "It sounds like a popularity contest, but it isn't," an official insists. The process . . . improves productivity and keeps employee relations at an even keel.*
>
> *All candidates are screened by Delta to make sure they meet FAA and company requirements. The airline also reserves the right to reject the worker choice. But "it very, very rarely has," a spokesman asserts. In some 50 elections staged each year, an official says, "90 percent of the time they pick the same people we would."*
>
> *The process may not work well for other companies, a spokesman says, but "it works well for us."*
>
> — Wall Street Journal[3]

their frequent differences of opinion, coupled with their high willingness to work together in an attempt to find a mutually agreeable solution. Opponents will allow us to tell our story.

Bedfellows are those whom we may agree with on an issue but don't trust. Congress is a good example of a place where bedfellow deals are made daily between people with mutual interests, but not necessarily mutual trust. Forging agreements between bedfellows demands specificity in place of trust. We may need clear written agreements spelling out precisely what each side has promised.

Adversaries are those with whom we share little trust or agreement. Other than giving compromise with adversaries your best shot, there is little you can do. Although you should always consider what the other party will get out of a compromise, it is especially critical to do so with adversaries. You must put yourself in their shoes and try to find reasons why they might benefit from your idea.

Fence sitters are those people who don't let us know where they stand. They may nod assent today, and rescind it tomorrow. Contracts were invented for these people.

Just think of all the good ideas that have died in your organization simply because someone failed to gain the support of other interested individuals or groups. As difficult as it may seem to talk with fence sitters or adversaries, you have little choice.

Give a specific charge. Make certain the steering committee understands the limits of its charge. It may be something like, "to assist in planning and monitoring a process that will increase involvement of staff with the goal of improving overall quality within the branch." You are not necessarily giving the committee an equal vote with you, nor are you abdicating your responsibility as manager. You are simply using this committee to help you think through the issues and suggest ways of proceeding.

Partnerships and the Road to Hell

Watch for these traps in your move toward a partnership approach.

Father knows best. The organization or the individual manager makes the decisions that affect the lives of the staff. Children resent this parental approach; think how adults must react to it.

Insincere gestures. If the process is merely a way to gain concessions or an attempt to weaken unions by dissipating skills within a larger work group, people will soon recognize the ploy.

Too much enthusiasm. Your enthusiasm about making changes may blind you to the fact that others may not share that enthusiasm. While you are celebrating, people are stewing over what you might be conjuring up for them.

Be sure to keep your viewpoint in balance. Have your staff or the steering committee assist you in working on all remaining steps in the planning process, such as holding a discussion on the organization's readiness for involvement (see Chapter 7), determining values, and developing an action plan.

7

Beginning the Discussion

I want to tell you to just live in the mess. Throw yourself out into the convulsions of the world. I'm not telling you to make the world better, because I don't believe progress is necessarily part of the package. I'm just telling you to live in it, to look at it, to witness it. Try and get it. Take chances, make your own work, take pride in it. Seize the moment.

— Joan Didion
Commencement Address[1]

Before proceeding with any plan to increase the partnership, you should assess the current situation. Just as a mountain climber needs to check weather conditions before beginning a perilous assault, so too should you check the climate or readiness of your work unit for these changes.

The simplest way to assess the work unit is to hold a discussion with a few trusted colleagues. Pull together people who can give you a full picture of the work unit. This meeting might, for instance, include other managers, representatives of any particular interests within the work unit, and some customers and suppliers to give a needed outsider's perspective. At the very least, you should invite members of your steering committee.

Ask people to bring documents that may have some bearing on the conversation. You might consider the results of a recent employee attitude survey, the CEO's statement of values and direction, or a report measuring customer satisfaction.

Encourage candid discussion of the issues. You are looking for information that will help you identify practices that support involvement or highlight potential trouble spots.

Starting Points

The conversation topics listed below should help you focus the discussion on issues that can either help or hinder the employee involvement process. Each category lists a positive and a negative statement. Consider these as ends of a continuum. Your organization and work unit will fall somewhere on that scale. For example, if managers at Eastern Airlines had examined the category "management/staff history" in the late 1980s, they would most likely have placed a mark near the low end of the scale, then explained the reason for the score.

1___2 X 3____4____5____6____7____8____9____10
Negative   Positive

Explanation of Score:

Two major strikes in the past few years. During early days of the machinists' strike, two other unions walked out in sympathy. Former chairman Frank Borman's well-publicized disdain of employee involvement: "I'm not going to have the monkeys running the zoo."[2]

Management/Staff History

Positive. The organization and this unit have enjoyed a long history of good management/staff (labor) relations.

Negative. Management/staff relations have been tense for a long time. Trust is low on both sides. Suspicion is high whenever management tries something new.

1___2___3___ 4___5___6___7___8___9___10
Negative   Positive

Explanation of Score:

Organizational Structure

Positive. Senior management encourages a flexible organizational structure. They may direct individual work units to create formal or informal systems that serve the task. Work units are organized in ways that increase quality and efficiency. People are encouraged to cross organizational boundaries or jump levels in the organization to get the job done.

Negative. The organization is highly bureaucratic. Titles and the chain of command are strictly adhered to. Turf wars may reign between departments.

1___2___3___ 4___5___6___7___8___9___10
Negative   Positive

Explanation of Score:

Values and Vision

Positive. Senior management offers a clear and consistent message of values and vision, and these statements are consistent with the principles of employee involvement. Senior management champions these values and promotes their use to inform the actions throughout the organization.

Negative. If senior management provides any statement of vision, it is generally believed to be only lip service. Organizational practices, despite words to the contrary, largely reflect Theory X.

1___2___3___4___5___6___7___8___9___10
Negative   Positive

Explanation of Score:

Communication

Positive. The organization encourages open communication. In keeping with the maxim that truth can come from anywhere, no restriction is put on a person's freedom to criticize or suggest. All employees are given information about the organization's performance in open forums — such as quarterly meetings with question and answer sessions and discussions about the anticipated direction the organization may take. An honest attempt is made to address rumors. People receive timely and helpful feedback.

Negative. Information is closely held. Often even those with a practical need to know don't get the information required to make informed decisions. People are frequently in the dark with regard to their own performance.

1____2____3____4____5____6____7____8____9____10
Negative   Positive

Explanation of Score:

Customer Focus

Positive. The organization bases its evaluation of performance on the customers' reactions to products and services. This customer orientation extends to external as well as internal customers.

Negative. Evaluations are internal. Each unit evaluates its own performance based on internal criteria, such as the information services department that rates its work based on its own perceptions rather than on evaluations by the recipients of the service. The organization may blame customers for its own failures.

1____2____3____4____5____6____7____8____9____10
Negative   Positive

Explanation of Score:

Skills

Positive. The people of this work unit have the skills needed to serve customers well. The staff are capable of identifying problems, working on practical solutions, anticipating needs, and completing the highest quality of work without close supervision.

Negative. For any number of reasons, people lack the training to do the job right or take on greater responsibility.

        1____2____3____4____5____6____7____8____9____10
        Negative   Positive

Explanation of Score:

Commitment

Positive. Senior management has shown real commitment to the process of employee involvement. They provide direction, resources, and support for managers and work units that attempt to apply more participatory approaches.

Negative. Employee involvement is believed to be just a passing fad, a "flavor of the month." Few take the talk of participation seriously.

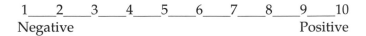

        1____2____3____4____5____6____7____8____9____10
        Negative   Positive

Explanation of Score:

Driving Force

Positive. Some external driving force is pushing the organization to examine its practices regarding quality and service. For instance, the company may be facing severe competition from Japanese manufacturing or anticipating a new threat to markets from the European community.

Negative. There is nothing pushing improvement at this time. A large government bureaucracy may believe it is immune from public calls for higher quality, or a company may believe that it has no serious competition and therefore no reason to change.

1___2___3___4___5___6___7___8___9___10
Negative   Positive

Explanation of Score:

Manager's Role

Positive. Managers and supervisors are expected to provide participatory leadership. They are given training and encouragement to involve people to a greater degree.

Negative. Managers are rewarded solely on bottom-line performance. They may be encouraged to monitor the work of staff very closely, and are held accountable if a staff member takes a risk and fails.

1___2___3___4___5___6___7___8___9___10
Negative   Positive

Explanation of Score:

Quality and Service Standards

Positive. The organization has clear and specific ways by which to measure quality and service. Quality, not quantity, is valued. When a problem occurs, staff are encouraged to find the real reason for the breakdown and correct it without laying blame on anyone. The organization encourages people to continually seek ways to improve processes.

Negative. The organization measures quantity — items produced, numbers served, time spent processing a complaint. Or it may respond to quality or service problems with a crisis response — solving a particular problem, but failing to examine the real causes of the problem. Often management searches for a scapegoat.

```
1____2____3____4____5____6____7____8____9____10
Negative                                    Positive
```

Explanation of Score:

Rewards

Positive. People are rewarded for doing high-quality work. These rewards, which are valued by employees, may include monetary incentives such as bonuses or profit sharing, or may be non-monetary recognition such as awards, parties, or even management-served breakfasts.

Negative. People do not believe they are given credit or recognition for their work. If a system of rewards is in place, it is commonly viewed with skepticism.

```
1___2___3___4___5___6___7___8___9___10
```
Negative   Positive

Explanation of Score:

Performance Review

Positive. Performance review is used primarily as a tool to help plan for the future. Weaknesses are used as opportunities to consider corrective actions. Candid feedback is encouraged from boss to employee, among peers, between work units, and from employee to boss. Performance review is simply a discussion between adults; no one receives a report card with a performance grade on it.

Negative. Performance review is wasteful and demeaning. Quotas are assigned specifying how many employees can receive higher ratings. Individuals, not teams, are rated. Bosses rate subordinates, never the reverse. These number ratings may be used as criteria for determining pay increases. The review process is used primarily to examine past performance rather than as a tool for dealing with the future.

```
1___2___3___4___5___6___7___8___9___10
```
Negative   Positive

Explanation of Score:

Joy

Positive. People truly enjoy working here. Morale, camaraderie among staff, and fun are a way of life.

Negative. This is a world of False X's. People go through the motions and do what they are asked, but for them it is "just a job."

1____2____3____4____5____6____7____8____9____10
Negative   Positive

Explanation of Score:

Once all of the above categories have been discussed, consider the following questions:

- How much support can I expect from senior management if we begin the process of increasing participation?
- What obstacles can I anticipate if we proceed?
- What power do I have to remove obstacles?

Even though a factor such as "commitment" may seem entirely out of your control, push yourself to consider ways in which you might exert some influence over it. For example, even if upper management lacks commitment to employee involvement, does that necessarily mean that you could not create a vision and direction for your unit that would increase participation?

Subsequent chapters should help you begin to address the issues raised during this discussion that are within your control to influence.

8

Identifying the Values

Few things are harder to put up with than the annoyance
of a good example.

— Mark Twain

One of the fundamental truths of Buddhism is that life is difficult. If it were easy, we wouldn't need religion. We'd simply spend one Sunday in church, get the picture, and from that moment on lead lives consistent with our beliefs. Unfortunately, life bombards us with challenges that cause us to seek renewal. We may attend church, read self-help books, or walk in the woods, not so much to find new ideas, but to find courage and guidance to live by values we hold dear.

Working with people — a significant part of a manager's life — is difficult too. The Road to Hell beckons at every turn. At times it may seem that everything works against the ideal of true partnership between management and staff. It is the magnitude of these challenges that may make us cry, "What's the use?" Treating each other well in heaven would be easy, but treating each other with dignity and respect in a less-than-heavenly world demands our constant attention.

This chapter asks you, in cooperation with your staff or your steering committee, to identify the values on which you want to anchor your relationships. We will look at the mundane everyday world where our values are tested ceaselessly in the ways in which we listen and speak, criticize and support, and struggle between candor and more political responses. Most of us can live by our values when the big challenges face us; it is the thousands of seemingly insignificant "moments of truth" that erode our good intent.

The Values of Involvement

In organizations where participation and commitment are high, you find people actively struggling to live by common values. This fact is easy to miss. When American industry realized that the Japanese were doing something different, they assumed that the technique of quality circles was a key reason for their success. In some ways, they were right; the circle was an important tool. Unfortunately, many organizations tried to graft the Japanese cherry onto American elms, with dismal results. A value like acknowledging the importance of listening to the people closest to the product was foreign to American management practice, and the new branches often died.

In organizations where quality circles do work, you will find far more than the sound techniques of the problem-solving group; you'll find managers and hourly workers living by shared values. These shared values are essential to their continued success. The techniques of involvement, whether achieved through circles or self-directed teams, work only if the values of involvement are firmly rooted.

One manufacturer initiated employee involvement like so many other American companies and, like its counterparts, watched the circles fail. It wasn't until management and union leadership met and identified mutual values and a common vision that the process began working. When managers and union representatives were asked to write down their respective visions for the company, it was impossible to tell the difference between the statements from the two groups. That was the turning point. As a result, the company's business expanded and the company became a preferred supplier to the major auto manufacturers.

Identifying the values. In Chapter 3 we examined themes that make work valuable. For most, it is a combination of meaning, results, challenge, respect and recognition, control, and affiliation. When these qualities are integral parts of our work, the organization wins by seeing a high commitment to quality and service, and we win by knowing that our work is more than a job — it is something that gives meaning to our lives.

You and your staff or steering committee should identify the values or qualities that you want to inform your work together. Your list of common values might include the following:

- We pay attention to quality over quantity.
- We consider our customers and suppliers to be our team members.
- We treat each other with respect.
- We encourage the development of everyone's skills.
- We encourage each other to take educated risks.
- We believe in giving and receiving candid feedback.
- We play our cards face up, giving each other straight-forward information.
- We listen to and consider the opinions of all team members.

The Levi Strauss company distributes embossed paperweights that read, "We want satisfaction from accomplishments, balanced personal and professional lives, and to have fun in our endeavors." NCR Corporation emphasizes "an environment in which employees' creativity and productivity are encouraged, recognized, valued, and rewarded."[1]

Among Progressive Casualty Insurance Company's core values are integrity and the Golden Rule. I was skeptical. Did anybody in the company know that the Golden Rule was one of its core values? If so, did anybody care? Was it stitched on samplers hanging in the homey offices of marketing MBAs? My cynicism was misplaced. The core values have become touchstones in meetings regarding all manner of issues. Occasionally, someone will stop a discussion and say, "Wait a minute. What we are considering seems to go against our core values." Sometimes the values are used to reconsider a decision or to critique decisions made by other divisions.

Is this easy for them to do? No, of course not. Do they do it perfectly? No, they are human just like us, struggling with the challenges of doing business. Sometimes they may fail in their resolve, but the values bring them back home. The values help guide future actions and give a reference point by which to examine past practices.

Giving the acid test. It is easy to create a list of nice-sounding values. Some of the worst places have some of the most inspiring slogans. What distinguishes the best from the worst is the ability to turn values into action. You must find ways to use the values of partnership to inform your day-to-day decisions and activities.

Debate how these values will be used. Apply the values to the most mundane events. Discuss how these values would come into play in such pedestrian activities as running meetings, resolving conflicts, considering people for promotion or special assignments, or working with suppliers and customers. Aldous Huxley felt that Dostoyevski was a far more profound thinker than Kierkegaard, because he was able to make ideas come alive in concrete form through his stories. Kierkegaard, a pure philosopher, remained abstract and never dealt with the challenge of putting ideals to the test in the real world. Struggling with the question of how values can come alive helps us turn abstract concepts into concrete actions.

You might consider the following questions. How will these values come into play as we:

- work with our customers and suppliers?
- make decisions?
- try to resolve differences of opinion?
- are faced with deadlines that could undercut quality?
- allocate resources?
- reward and recognize good work?

To ensure that values rise above mere platitudes, perhaps one more value should be added to the list: a commitment to applying the values every day.

Many organizations have a list of core values. Never mind those, develop your own. Your unit's list should complement and even overlap the corporate words and phrases, but it is important that your unit develop a list of values that it believes in. No one else can tell your unit how to bring these qualities to life in the thousands of little opportunities that arise every day.

The Manager's Special Role Regarding Values

Practicing what you preach. People will look to you for guidance. Is the boss trying to apply the values? If not, don't expect others to. This may be difficult, but consider the manager Marcus Aurelius. While emperor of the Roman Empire, he faced wars with northern Barbarians, plague, and severe economic troubles. And still, by campfire, after grueling days of battle, he wrote the *Meditations*, his guide to himself on how he should live. The struggle he faced — that we all face — is how to live by those ideals we value no matter what challenges confront us. Stepping back periodically, if even for a moment, to reflect on our beliefs and on how we live helps us come ever closer to matching our actions to our values.

Eliminating hassles. If you want people to live by these values, you must help remove hassles. Most of the chapters in this book examine ways of finding the hassles that inhibit partnership and eliminating them. The key is your willingness to always look for ways to help the unit practice living by its values.

Injecting new life into old, tired values. You may have a vision statement regarding involvement or quality that is good, but is gathering dust. The vision may be all right, but there is no commitment to it. For example, one school system routinely put out visions of quality in the form of posters. They were displayed in hallways and some classrooms and that was that. No one ever mentioned them. No teacher was ever asked what he or she thought of them. No discussion was ever given to turning these goals into action. They were empty, forgotten words.

If you suffer from empty words, get your staff together and 'fess up. Tell them that you believe quality, service, and partnership are worthy goals and that you want their help in making the vision come alive. Let people know that you are committing time and energy to ensuring that the vision becomes reality.

Values on the Road to Hell

Beware of these pitfalls in trying to live by your highest values.

A discussion of values turns into a gripe session. Sometimes, instead of focusing on the future and possibilities for improvement, a meeting degenerates into complaining about all the things that are wrong and all the reasons why things will never get any better. Think in terms of possibilities. Keep the focus on what could be.

The all-encompassing dream. Keep the discussions focused on involvement. This is not a strategic planning session, merely a meeting to begin the process of improving the ways you work together.

Father still knows best. Too often, leaders initiate new programs in a paternalistic manner. The boss comes in and announces what the vision or value of the month will be. Sometimes that is the only way to do it, but you run the risk of creating resistance to an otherwise thoughtful move.

"Feel-good" values. Without a focus on bottom-line issues such as quality and service, the values discussion could become quite "warm and fuzzy" — and impractical. As you bask in the sun, you may fail to notice the storm gathering just offshore.

Just assume that everyone on your team is human and will err. There will be days when it will seem like no one remembers the values. Old quarrels will rear their ugly heads; "us versus them" blaming and gossip will spread; you might even make a decision that angers everyone. Expect it. The most important difference between the old days and the present time is that today you have shared values to help you assess the situation and get back on track.

9

Pulling It All Together

First we will be best, then we will be first.

— Lou Holtz
Head Football Coach, Notre Dame[1]

Once you and your steering committee or staff have examined the issues in Chapter 7, "Beginning the Discussion," you should be able to see what it will take to build a partnership between management and the employees. Now it is time to begin planning.

Making Sense of the Assessments

Undoubtedly you have identified issues in the assessments included in chapters 5 and 7 that will help you implement more effective employee involvement processes as well as issues that could create major obstacles for you. Use a force-field analysis to help you sort out the positive from the negative.

A force-field analysis is a problem-solving tool that helps identify the relative importance of forces working for and against you.[2] Whenever you consider a goal, or are faced with a problem, competing forces work against each other, some pushing you toward resolution, others driving you away. When these competing forces are in balance, they make progress difficult, but also keep things from getting too much worse.

One division director in a large organization realized that partnership would have to begin at her level, since senior management seemed interested only in giving it lip service. In spite of this potential obstacle, however, she decided to proceed. A number of things work in her favor: She enjoys a high degree of support from her branch managers and staff members, another division in the company has had some success in increasing participation, training dollars are available, and the need to try something different is critical.

Working against her are senior management's tepid support for such efforts and her fear that their support could be withdrawn at any time, her own lack of skills with regard to leading an involvement process, the division's skepticism over this new fad, and a lack of time.

As the manager and the steering committee weigh the positive and the negative, they begin to get a clearer picture of the forces that push against each other as they attempt to change their work environment. The discussion turns to the relative weight of the various forces and determining where they might have impact using a positive force to their advantage, or reducing the impact of a negative one.

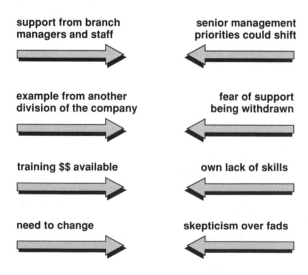

After examining the competing forces, the committee decides that it can have sufficient impact on enough forces to proceed. If it uses the existing support from managers and staff to allay skepticism, establishes a relationship with the successful division to learn about the process, gets immediate training for the division director, and uses the director's ideas on ways she might get the CEO to bless the process, then the committee might succeed.

Applying force to positive factors and diminishing the force of the negative will move the force field to the right, closer to the goal. Even if the strategies don't get the group all the way to the goal, any significant movement to the right should improve the feeling of partnership in the office.

Here are the steps to use:

1. *Write down the aim or goal — the reason you are doing this.* It might read, "To increase our unit's commitment to quality and service to our customers and to ourselves."

2. *List all the forces that could potentially push you toward your goal.* Although the example listed just a few forces, examine all your documents and think back over discussions to create a complete list of forces.

3. *List all the forces working against you.* Once again, be as thorough as possible.

4. *Assign weights to all the items on both lists.* 10 = a potentially important force, 1 = an insignificant force. You might rate the CEO's commitment to high involvement a "4" if past behavior makes you question his or her sincerity regarding this issue.

5. *Circle those items over which you could exert some control to increase or diminish the force.* Some forces may rank "10" on the negative side and yet be out of your control. Perhaps the promotion policy within the company is terrible and works against your best efforts to provide opportunities for your team, and you have no control over making it a fairer process. Better to acknowledge its potential force, and put your resources into increasing or diminishing those forces where you do have some control.

6. *Examine the list.* Given the magnitude of the lists and the relative weights of various forces, ask yourself if the goal is realistic. If so, proceed. If not, redefine the goal to make it more realistic. For instance, say you realize that the forces against real participation are strong and pretty much out of your control. You work in a large bureaucracy that demands 17 levels of signatures on every decision, management's authority is undercut on even the most mundane decisions, people are fired for taking risks, and so on. And on the positive side, you read this book. Redefine your goal. A more realistic goal might be to create a work environment in which all people live by a core set of values, such as treating each other with dignity and respect. After all, you don't need corporate support to treat people decently.

7. *Looking at the items on both sides that have the most potential force, determine which items your team will tackle.* Although many forces may have a strong impact, your limited resources may dictate that you apply your energy to just a few.

8. *Develop strategies for working on the forces you selected.* Knowledge of other organizations' efforts will serve you well at this stage. Learn how others have confronted the negative force of senior management teams that only give lip service to involvement. How have others built on the organization's willingness to put dollars and other resources behind involvement efforts? How have other branch chiefs instituted these processes even when their bosses have worked against them?

The Plan

Based on the values you identified in the last chapter and the strategies you just created for working on the competing forces, write an action plan. This need not be a long document. It is simply a working guide to help you and your steering committee bring this process to life. Here, in loose chronological order, are some steps to consider:

Write down the aim. Write down the same goal or aim as for the force-field analysis.

List the values. The values indicate how you want to work together to achieve the aim. Include them here as a reminder, and to help employees who may join you later understand where you want to go.

> *Make no little plans; they have no magic to stir men's blood.*
>
> — Daniel Hudson Burnham
> Architect of the Flatiron Building,
> the first American skyscraper

Build support within the unit. If your unit is large, determine how you will bring others into this process. No matter how noble your intent, if people aren't involved in the early stages, you risk failure.

Build support among stakeholders. Identify all others who have a stake in how you work. These could be groups such as customers, senior managers, other units in the organization, the general public, and suppliers. Determine their stake in your success and assess their willingness to support you. If support is low, attempt to find ways to make the process attractive to them. (See Chapter 6 for more information on this.)

Identify strategies for increasing positive forces. Create strategies for increasing those positive forces that you believe can help you.

But consider the potential opposite and equal reaction if your strategy pushes against a strong negative force.

Identify strategies for reducing negative forces. Lessening negative forces may be more difficult initially, but may serve you better since it seldom invokes such a strong counter-reaction.

Learn from experts. Identify the experts who can help you. Experts are those who have gone before and can give you sage advice. As I mentioned above, they can help you look at the force-field analysis, but they can also suggest approaches to involvement. Ask tough questions and listen to their answers. If you can't meet with them, call them. Most people are delighted to talk about their successes. (During the development of this book, no one ever turned down my request to ask them about how they initiated successful employee participation processes.) People take pride in their successes. Use that to your advantage.

Use these contacts to learn more about options. Don't rush into a way of improving without shopping around. Don Morrison of AVCO Financial Services said he spent a year reading, visiting, and debating ("What would continuous improvement look like here? What do we mean by involvement? Does it mean that everyone has a say in every single decision?"). Don and his senior staff knew that ideas could come from anywhere, not just from financial institutions, so they visited organizations as diverse as Japanese manufacturing facilities and a Southern textile mill.

Build a network with these people. One way to begin is to attend one of the many conferences given on employee participation. Look for conferences where representatives from organizations talk about their own successes and failures.

Create a step-by-step pilot test plan. (Save this step until you have started working on the previous step.) Assume that the best-laid plans will run into trouble. Things will not go as smoothly as you had hoped. Consider yourself on a steep learning curve; mistakes and setbacks are merely learning opportunities. Without this learner's attitude, a major problem may be enough to convince you that these things can't possibly work.

If you begin the process slowly or in a selected portion of the work unit, you will have an opportunity to contain potential problems and work the bugs out of the prototype.

In the pilot, describe the process you will use to improve quality and involvement. (This book focuses on the partnership side of the equation; you must balance that with a sound method for improving and measuring quality. Appendix A suggests many resources to consider.)

- Determine the roles of all players.
- Identify the ways in which you will measure success.
- Describe how you will monitor progress.
- Determine how people will be rewarded for success.
- Build in "small wins."
- Determine how you will keep senior management and other stakeholders informed.

During the learning stage everyone will be trying out new skills. The manager may be trying to learn how to facilitate a team, others may be trying to find ways to come to the boss with candid negative reports. You won't be perfect at it; just accept that fact and learn from it.

The Road to Hell. Before beginning the pilot, address the following issues to avoid trouble down the road:

1. Have we considered all of the steps in this plan as thoroughly as we should? Are we moving too quickly?
2. Are we excited about proceeding? If not, why? Do not proceed until you have resolved this issue. Perhaps you are doing this because someone else thinks it's a good idea. If so, you already know how easy it will be to sabotage this process.
3. Are there any other potential Road to Hell issues that could hurt us?

Encourage continuous improvement. As with quality, you will never arrive at an end point with regard to involvement. Continuous improvement is essential. A vital quality circle process may lose steam after a few years and people may wish for a greater degree of involvement on a day-to-day basis. This should not frighten managers. If anything, they should be delighted that their teams want more authority and responsibility.

Pay attention to the ways in which you will ensure that the partnership remains alive and vital. Your plan is written on paper, not stone tablets, so consider it something that can be changed when needed. Conditions will change or you may learn new and better ideas that should cause you to erase and alter. Keep the document informal; don't have it typeset. Write a plan that begs to be used and debated.

PART THREE

Keeping It Alive

10

Providing Direction

[The best managers] are willing to follow their hunches. They usually work off informed hunches that something is timely or opportune and they're willing to operate on that hunch before all the facts are in. They are the natural experimenters (or explorers) in the business — they are the Marco Polos. They judiciously take risks and take them for reasons they can describe to you. It is their demonstration of what can be done that galvanizes the rest of the organization.

— Nancy Badore
Executive Director
Ford Executive Development Center

Managers in a division of one Fortune 500 company cannot state how their work fits into the corporation's strategic vision. These managers are bright, committed, hard-working people, but they simply don't know how or if their work contributes to the health of the company. Consequently, in the absence of corporate direction, they created their own. When asked if they are productive, the answer is a resounding yes. Perhaps they are. If the company is lucky — if the division has guessed correctly — then it will play a vital role in helping meet the corporation's strategic goals.

Imagine a fleet traveling through heavy fog without radio contact. When the fog eventually lifts, the ships may be together, or they may be scattered across many oceans. That shrouded approach to direction could cost them dearly.

The "heavy fog" phenomenon occurs at every level of organizations, from boardrooms to stockrooms. When fog rolls in, we make our best guess, then set sail. We need direction; it could be as broad as the statement, "Use your best judgment when you work with customers," or as specific as the grid used by BBC directors to tell actors precisely when and where to move.

Ambiguous direction turns work into a guessing game as we attempt to interpret meaning from faulty signals. Does the fact that the boss didn't mention anything in the staff meeting mean that she is happy with the project? Life is confusing enough without fretting over what the boss meant by what was said, unclearly communicated, or left unsaid. Part of your job is to reduce confusion. Don't expect people to divine your intentions — tell them what they are.

We tend to believe we are better at this than we are. Gary Latham and Edwin Locke conducted a series of experiments on goal setting in organizations.[1] Although managers were skeptical of their research — after all, hadn't they been setting goals for years? — they allowed the researchers to conduct their work. Surprisingly, many people told them, "I've been working here for ten years, and this is the first time I've known what I was supposed to do." They noted that productivity rose, on average, by 17 percent in the companies that worked with them to clarify or define performance goals.

Direction may take many forms, from giving instructions to setting the tone that demonstrates how people should treat each other. This chapter addresses those issues.

Direction Regarding the Task

Robert Waterman uses the phrase "directed autonomy." I like that idea; it is a worthy goal. People need to be given direction and then given the freedom to make choices that help accomplish the goal. According to Waterman, "The manager's job is to establish the boundaries around a fairly broad solution space. The individual's responsibility is to find the best way of doing things within that space."[2]

However, we must realize that circumstances won't always allow us to use "directed autonomy" to the extent we might wish. Think of direction as a continuum. At the left end is a point of maximum direction on your part. At the far right end of the continuum is a point at which an employee needs very little direction.

<--->

Maximum Direction   Minimum Direction

Say you are working with a new employee. You will probably need to give specific instructions regarding quality and service standards and procedures. You may need to show samples of high-quality work or ways of measuring quality. You will need to refine your directions as the person works, bending here and there to make certain he or she understands precisely what you want.

On the other hand, when an employee knows the job, knows the expectations, and holds a high commitment to quality, direction should be minimal. Thomas Jefferson knew that his personal secretary, Meriwether Lewis, was capable of planning for and leading an expedition into the newly purchased lands west of the Mississippi. He didn't tell Lewis how to do the job; he simply wrote, "The object of your mission is to explore the Missouri River, and such principal stream [sic] of it, as, by its course and communication with the water of the Pacific Ocean may offer the most direct and practicable water communication across this continent for the purposes of commerce." Simple and direct. The directive that opened the Northwest to exploration uses a scant 47 words.

Although your goal as leader is to move as far right as possible, the reality is that there will be times when you need to operate at various points along the scale. When a highly skilled employee takes on a new assignment, he or she may need very specific guidance. During a time when the central office is demanding a rush order, you may need to take a directive approach with an otherwise efficient group simply because the task demands that one person call the shots during the crisis.

The need for direction changes as people develop skills, confidence, and commitment. The leader must know when to direct and when to step back and allow people to call their own shots. Obviously, someone new to a task needs more direction and feedback than someone with more knowledge and experience. The amount and quality of direction can be considered in three broad areas.*

Stage 1	Stage 2	Stage 3
Orientation	Apprenticeship	Mastery

Stage One. Orientation to the job. The person new to the organization or new to a task may need considerable guidance. Build a structure where it is impossible for him or her to fail.

Stage Two. Apprenticeship. The employee understands the work of the unit, who the players are, and where to get the best coffee in the building. Now he or she is ready to begin a process of job mastery. He or she needs your guidance.

Stage Three. Mastery. People who have reached this level know the job well — they are masters at it. You should be able to give them the broadest parameters within which to work. Mastery should be your goal. Work is best when people know what to do, can take corrective action themselves, and can work hassle-free. This is directed autonomy. See the next section for steps in delegating to masters.

How much direction is too much? Here are a few guidelines for gauging your level of direction.

Ask them. Ask people if they are getting the information they need to do the job, then stop and listen to what they say. Too often

---

* See Chapter 14 for detailed guidelines regarding management practices at all levels of development.

direction is a one-way communication — perhaps a memo that the employee must translate and make sense of. Direction is better if it's a dialogue; give the direction then make sure the person understands. Discuss it. Memos are poor substitutes for face-to-face communication.

Oh, yeah! Apply the "Oh, yeah!" test. When the employee's look brightens, and he or she smiles and says, "Oh, yeah, I see what you want," then perhaps you've given enough direction.

Keep it simple. Scott Markey of Progressive Casualty Insurance decided to reduce the number of objectives assigned to subordinates from 25 to five or six. He realized that if he had difficulty juggling that many objectives, then others might too. Simplicity allows people to focus on the essentials.

Delegating to Masters

Organizations seldom allow a manager to squander raw materials, yet they will allow and (sometimes even encourage) managers to waste the talents of valuable human resources. Whenever oversight is too extensive, or a manager "helps out" when not really needed, he is wasting the time and talent of people. In short, he is costing the company money. This extravagance is one of the deadliest Road to Hell factors. People with talent, skills, and commitment should be allowed to shine. They can make good decisions, spot problems, and take corrective action.

When people have the skills and commitment to do the job right, the manager should search for every opportunity to delegate responsibility and authority to them. These people are your greatest resource.

There are many reasons why delegation is not used effectively, but high on the list (if not topping the list) is fear. Organizations are afraid of delegating responsibility. Although most of us trust our own ability to make decisions, we often doubt that ability in our colleagues. This creates an environment in which important decisions must be approved and reapproved ad infinitum. Often this

The British Broadcasting Company consistently produces extraordinary television shows, such as "I, Claudius" and the Masterpiece Theatre series, seen on public television in the United States. A significant reason for their consistency is the way in which they prepare for productions.

The director takes full responsibility for the realization of the script. Everyone working on the production — sound, costumes, lighting, set designer — works with the director in pre-production meetings. The director explains his or her vision of the show. Members of the team are expected to read the script many times. The director keeps pushing — asking them about how they will convey the meaning through costumes, through lighting, etc. The experts in each of these areas are expected to add their ideas to the overall plan.

The director plots every camera angle and every move the actors will take on a grid before the cast and crew begin production. So instead of telling a camera operator to "zoom in on Claudius," he or she will receive written instructions on the script to "move camera to coordinate G-3, move in medium-close on Claudius." The camera operator knows precisely where he or she needs to be at every moment, and within that framework has the freedom to make suggestions and use creative judgment.

Every member of the team receives a copy of the marked-up script that includes all blocking (actors' moves), camera shots, light and sound cues and anything else that seems important. Everyone on the set works from the same document. This minimizes confusion and eliminates the need to give minute directions during shooting. (Time on the sound stage is the most expensive time for a production team; actions that save time here save money.)

Rehearsals take place in a rehearsal hall replete with coordinates drawn on the floor. The assistant calls the shots using the common script, freeing the director to watch monitors and make certain the vision is working.

This procedure is in marked contrast to many other productions where everyone receives instructions orally during the shooting. This wastes time, is often chaotic, and allows the crew to focus their attentions elsewhere during the long delays. The detailed single document actually encourages ideas, since everyone is focused on the same activity.[3]

fear is so overwhelming that it becomes part of formal organizational procedure. Directives inform us of the Byzantine maze our decisions must travel before they are approved or rejected. This creates a paradox: we fail, not because we are careless, but because we are too careful.

Sadly, delegation is so uncommon that even organizations that want to push control to lower levels have great difficulty doing so. They don't know where to begin or how to support delegation when they do try to use it. When this occurs, they revert to old, "safe" practices.

The steps in delegating. There is a sequence for successfully handing over tasks to your employees.

Step 1: Commitment. None of the guidelines in this book will work without commitment. Organizations and managers must be committed to making delegation work. There is no secret to losing weight: simply take in fewer calories than you burn. Yet a fortune is made every year by "diet experts" who promise that their diet offers the secret to weight loss. These books sell because people lack the commitment to lose weight and look for an easy method. Delegation is no different. The tools for delegation are no secret, and are not even all that complex to apply — you probably know how to use them right now. Without commitment, these simple techniques cannot work.

Ask yourself:

- What are the advantages of delegating?
- How committed am I to delegating?
- What risks am I willing to take? (What if someone fails on a project? Will we end our noble experiment, or will we learn from the experience and continue using delegation as a tool?)

If you find that commitment to delegating is low, don't even try to delegate, because you'll fail.

Step 2: Assessing the situation. Delegation assumes trust. The leader trusts that the other person is committed to doing a good job and has the skills to make intelligent decisions. Trust should never be blind. You must assess the job and the person carefully. Ask yourself:

- What is the nature of this project or decision?
- What skills and information does someone need to complete the job effectively?
- Does this person have the background and commitment to do this job?

Step 3: Giving instructions. People need clear and specific guidelines. They need to know the boundaries: budget, time constraints, options you won't accept, options top management won't accept, and so forth.

Ask yourself:

- What background information does this person need to do the job?
- Is this assignment new or has the employee completed similar projects? If it is a new assignment, what special instructions or information must be given?
- What type of support is he or she likely to need during the project — a liaison to another office, advice, protection of time?

Step 4: Monitoring during the project. If you want good performance you must monitor the project. You never give up all control when you delegate. The buck still stops with you — there is no such thing as laissez-faire leadership in organizations. You should never be surprised by the final results.

Ask yourself:

- Is this person likely to know when to ask for help? If not, how often should I ask if he or she needs help?
- How much information do I need so I can sleep at night?

- If I have an open-door policy, will this person be likely to use it?
- What are the "red flags"? For example, how far can the time line slip before employees should tell me? What budget items should I hear about? What technical problems?

Step 5: Looking at the product. A project properly delegated and completed is cause for celebrating. Do so. A project that falls short should be examined closely to determine the exact reasons for failure. In all instances, you should analyze the process.

Ask yourself:

- Was the project a success? Why?
- Did the project fail? To what extent? Why?

Whether the project succeeded or failed, you should address the following:

- How clear were the initial instructions?
- How well did I monitor? Were there any places where the monitoring was less than adequate? Did I oversupervise the project?
- Did the employee have the time and resources to complete the job effectively?
- Was this assignment right for this employee?
- What were the pluses and minuses of the employee's performance?
- What were the pluses and minuses of my performance?
- What lessons did we learn that can serve us on future assignments?

Delegation is tough. Any time you give responsibility to another person and allow decisions to be made without constant oversight, you run the risk of failure. If you don't take these risks, however, you will never fully use the capabilities and resources of your staff.

Direction Regarding the Values

The champion of values. Ralph Waldo Emerson said that an organization is nothing more than the lengthened shadow of a single man. Although the larger organization has a real impact on what you do and how you do it, the spirit of involvement may live or die in your unit based on your actions. You will have an extraordinary influence over those who report to you. Employee involvement staff at an automobile manufacturing plant tell me that in every case, the success or failure of their quality circle teams can be predicted by the attitude and actions of the team supervisor. No exceptions. Those who support involvement make their support known, and people respond — even in environments where labor-management relationships have been poor.

Many organizations talk about "walking the talk." It is not enough to memorize the litany of correct things to say — you must live those values. People see through words. In the classic movie *It's a Gift*, W.C. Fields's son questioned his father's love after being denied a request. Fields raised his hand as if to slap the boy, bellowing, "He's not going to tell me I don't love him." It is this disparity between word and deed that causes confusion. Did the character love his son or didn't he? It is hard to tell.

Don Morrison, president of AVCO Financial Services, is someone who has made a profound change in how he works with people. Once a temperamental decision maker with more concern for product than process, he has become a champion of increased quality through involvement. Some still wait expectantly for the "old" Don to appear. If he loses his temper or makes an insistent demand, it is a sure sign to some that the "real" Don has returned.

To spend time with Don is to realize that he believes in the values of involvement and cares deeply about people. Yet his challenge is to continue *living* the values of involvement. This does not mean that he can no longer make autocratic decisions — he is the president, after all. But he does have a responsibility to make decisions that show he respects the dignity and wisdom of his staff. Although employee involvement encourages participation from all, it does not equate total — one person, one vote — democracy. He must live with this paradox and accept the fact that some may always be skeptical, just waiting for him to slip.

Managers must act consistently with the values of participation and look for ways to be active champions of it. Those who are successful at overcoming resistance to involvement look for opportunities to recognize initiative, encourage people to make their own decisions, and articulate the values of involvement.

Ricardo Semler, head of Semco, the Brazilian manufacturing plant mentioned earlier, turned his plant into a model of democracy. When the line employees suggested a location for a new plant that would be across the street from a company that had constant labor-management problems, senior management got scared. To buy the building might invite labor unrest at Semco; not to buy it would be to go against the values Semler espoused. "With two tough unions of our own, we weren't looking forward to front-row seats for every labor dispute that came along. But we accepted the employees' decision, because we believe that in the long run, letting people participate in the decisions that affect their lives will have a positive effect on employee motivation and morale."* They bought the building, the employees designed the layout, and productivity rose over 100 percent.[4] Semler's living commitment to espoused values is a dramatic example of "walking the talk."

Another example. If you believe training is essential to the improvement process, be the first to enroll. When Ford initiated its vision process, former chairman Donald Peterson was the first to sign up. Symbolic acts count for a lot, and Peterson's willingness to take time to attend this training sent a strong message to employees regarding his commitment.

The champion of quality. If you expect quality, then your staff should see that you settle for nothing less than top quality in your own work. If you expect people to remain calm when confronted

---

* Reprinted by permission of *Harvard Business Review*. An excerpt from "Managing without Managers" by Ricardo Semler (September/October 1989). Copyright © 1989 by the President and Fellows of Harvard College; all rights reserved.

by an irate customer, you must show your own ever-friendly, placid nature. We learn how to play the game by watching others. My favorite worldly philosopher, Yogi Berra, once said, "You can observe a lot just by watching."

Direction and the Road to Hell

Watch for a few danger areas in working to direct your employees' efforts.

Details to the 10th power. In some cases, rather than providing a direction, a leader will give the staff a massive pile of spirit-breaking directives. This guidance looks good on paper and it works well for programming robots, but it saps enthusiasm from real people.

Empty words. "Do as I say, not as I do" rings false. Partnership works when people believe that their leaders live by the values of partnership.

Direction is a combination of words and action. As a manager once told me, "We must not only practice what we preach, we must preach what we practice."

11

Keeping People Informed

Betty sure is going to be surprised when she sees her per-formance review in two months.

— A manager who shall remain nameless

If you want people to produce — to take responsibility and do the job right — you must give them timely information regarding where they stand. Tell them what you like, what you hate, what must be improved. That's feedback.

Giving feedback should be one of the simplest things a manager does. Just open your mouth and tell them what you think about their performance. Simple, right? Most of us think we do a fine job giving feedback; most of us are wrong. In fact, two-thirds of us are wrong.

When I conduct seminars on leadership, I ask participants a very simple question: How many of you receive adequate feedback? Generally only one-third raise their hands. This is incredible — something must be wrong. Feedback doesn't cost money; you don't need to spend money on new software or an expensive organizational analysis or anything else some outside expert might advise. You simply need to haul off and do it.

Without information on how they are doing, employees can't be expected to achieve very much. If you don't give people information on performance, you force them to invent their own assessments. Sometimes they'll be correct; sometimes they won't.

What to Do

Face it, feedback can be time-consuming. If you choose to ignore this critical activity, however, you may create a confused and frustrated staff. You also run the risk of work that doesn't measure up to your expectations.

Know the goal of the feedback. All performance feedback (with the possible exception of an exit interview) should be aimed toward helping someone perform the job better. You may need to discuss past mistakes in order to describe a problem, but then you must show what acceptable performance looks like and why it is important.

> *It's the manager's job to help employees get outstanding ratings.*
> — Department store manager

Do it now. Feedback must be given near the occurrence of the activity. Who can remember some specific action, whether positive or negative, six months later? The goal is to improve performance today — not six months from now.

Be specific. An expression like "great job" or "nice work" should not be confused with feedback. What was great about the job? What part of it made it so good? People need to know precisely what they did and did not do.

"Great job" is not a bad thing to say. People like to hear those words of encouragement, but that's what they are — encouragement. "Great job" lacks the specifics that will ensure continued stellar performance.

General statements when the message is negative — "you blew it this time, didn't you?" — should always be avoided. What did they blow? How bad was it? Was it a major gaffe? What will happen to them as a result? Will their friends and family ever speak to them again? General negative statements lead to paranoia.

Pick a suitable place. Some places are more conducive to hearing feedback than others. George Steinbrenner's method of telling the *New York Times* about his dissatisfaction with a Yankee player or manager was powerful, but a poor choice of venue for giving feedback.

Change the ratio. A child psychologist reports that parents give 25 reprimands for every positive comment they make to their children. If our ratio is 25:1 with people we love, what must it be with people we merely see at work? People do better when they receive positive and honest feedback. Look for opportunities to compliment and recognize good work. Don't just manage by exception and limit feedback to errors.

B.F. Skinner suggested that when the ratio is too strongly negative over positive, people quit working toward your goals and create their own goals. Those new goals, not surprisingly, are to avoid punishment. Under these conditions, people hide mistakes and cover up their actions, and as a result, quality suffers.

Four Types of Feedback

Not all feedback needs to take a lot of time or preparation. You can make it easier by identifying the type of feedback needed. These types include day-to-day, developmental, acid-bath, and team feedback.

Day-to-day feedback. Most feedback you give should fall into this category. Day-to-day feedback gives people timely information about where they stand. It allows you to correct problems as they occur, offer help, and encourage good performance. Here's how to do it.

Ask them what they need. A radical notion, but if you expect people to perform well without close supervision, then it makes sense to assume that they know what type of critique they need in order to perform well. Most people know what would help them do a better job, but aren't ever asked. Why not surprise them?

MBWA. Peters and Waterman coined the phrase "management by wandering around."[1] MBWA suggests that if you're out there you'll see what's going on and your staff will be able to call you aside to discuss their work.

- Set time aside to do this regularly. Make it a priority and put it on your list of things to do.
- Prime the pump. Don't wander around aimlessly, but ask questions about the work. Often those who report to us may know more about a particular subject or project than we do. Ask questions about it; you may learn something.
- Use the opportunity to praise work. (Reprimands should be given in private.)
- Spot-check and suggest small corrections.
- Keep your eyes open. You may see a need to change the directions you gave.

If you have trouble giving praise, you might make a list of things you want to say to individuals once you are out there.

When MBWA is impossible. Perhaps you're located far from your staff. (Another floor is not far; another city is far.)

- Use the phone or electronic mail. Check in. Ask how things are going. Ask if there is anything you can do to help.
- When distances are great, the chance for missed signals is great. Make certain you develop a method of keeping current with their work. When you have a question, don't wait for all the facts — that could take months. Check in with the person immediately.

Find ways to get information out to the people in a timely fashion. According to the *Wall Street Journal*, one General Motors assembly plant displays a large lighted sign that shows attendance figures, speed of the assembly line, and how well the plant is doing in comparison to another similar assembly plant. GM also gives workers access to warranty claims so they can see how well their work is holding up.[2] Although I can imagine some danger in such signs becoming a Big Brotherish way of pushing people, the idea — keeping people informed — does make sense.

Developmental feedback. New employees and people who are learning new tasks need lots of feedback. See Chapter 14, "Helping Employees Develop," for detailed ideas, but an outline of the main points to consider follows.

Meet. Hold frequent meetings to discuss progress on the development plan. Frequent may mean daily or it may mean weekly. You and the person developing the skill should decide together.

Encourage an open-door policy. Tell employees that you want them to come to you or to someone whom you've delegated whenever a problem occurs. Encourage them to take the initiative, and let them know you would rather they come too often than too seldom.

Use MBWA feedback. Make it easy for people to get advice and counsel.

Acid-bath feedback. This is the type of situation most of us dread. We have something very negative to say. We know the other person — the adversary — will respond in kind. These are the meetings that scare us off from giving feedback. Nothing will make an "acid-bath" meeting into a stroll through the park, but there are a few things you can do to increase your chances of survival.

Know what you want. Cato the Elder wrote, "Stick to the point and the words will take care of themselves." Often we forget our goal — which should be to improve performance — and instead allow the meeting to wander from topic to topic or get off track when one player attacks another.

In order to be able to stick to the point, you must first know what the point is. For instance, clients tell you that Jim is abrasive and they are considering changing vendors. Your goal, of course, is to point out the problem to Jim and gain his assurance that his performance will improve.

What do you know? Do you have evidence that supports your point? If not, get it. You must come to the meeting prepared with specific examples.

Anticipate the crazy stuff. You may have a scenario in mind. He'll say this, I'll say that, he'll say something else, then I'll throw in my most withering sarcasm to really nail him. When you hear yourself thinking up Hawkeye Pierce comebacks, resist that temptation to be brilliant. Save the retort for the novel you'll write someday.

By anticipating our own overreaction or underreaction, we increase our chances of overcoming the problems they bring. Typical problems that occur during the "acid-bath" meeting:

- You overstate the case in an effort to show the seriousness of the problem.
- You melt as the other person goes on the offensive and end by giving up.
- You allow the meeting to get sidetracked by arguing about your own performance or the performance of some third party.

Pay attention to these reactions and make an extra effort to keep the reason for the meeting foremost in your mind.

Timing. Pick a time and place that ensures privacy and will give you plenty of time to discuss the issues. Don't allow the meeting to be interrupted with phone calls or messages.

Context. Give them the context within which feedback occurs. Generally, are you satisfied with performance and do you consider this critical issue to be an exception? Or are you at wits' end and ready to fire the person?

A tough question. Could you be part of the problem? Ask about the extent to which you may be contributing to the problem by not giving adequate instruction, resources, or feedback. Be willing to take your share of the blame.

Look to the future. Focus on types of performance you would like to see in the future, and minimize the amount of time you spend on past performance. It is very difficult to be defensive about the future. State the problem, make sure the person understands what you are saying, then move on to ways of correcting the problem.

Keep the goal in mind — you want improved performance in the future, not in the past. Don't spend time trying to determine "who did what to whom." When you focus on the past, your goal changes to a far less productive one — "I've got to get him to cry 'uncle.'"

Listen, listen, listen. During the meeting listen to the employee's point of view. Listening does not imply that you agree; it simply means that you are willing to hear him or her out and change your mind if new information surfaces.

Determine action steps. Make certain that specific actions are identified during the meeting. What will this person do to correct the problem?

Stick to the point. Some believe you should mix positive with negative feedback. One teaspoon positive, then one teaspoon negative. I don't. If the feedback is negative, establish the context, stick to the point, and search for ways to improve performance.

Follow up. Schedule a follow-up meeting to take place sometime soon. I know the last thing you want to do is sit down with this person again, but a follow-up to check progress is essential.

Team Feedback. Often feedback should be directed to the full team. When work is productive, use the feedback meeting as an opportunity to identify the reasons that quality is so good; this helps the team learn and apply good practices to future work. When a project fails, the team should examine the reasons for the high rejection rate in order to make corrections.

Team feedback is practical and gives the entire team tools for doing the job better the next time. Here are some simple guidelines.

Overall assessment. Ask each team member to give a summary rating of the project. Limit responses to single phrases or words such as "so-so," "outstanding," and so forth. Or ask the team to assign a numerical rating — one for terrible, five for wonderful. This quick poll gives everyone common information regarding how the individuals involved view the project. Often you may find that some rate the team's work on the project high and others rate it low. This information primes the pump and provides a starting point for discussion.

What went right? Discuss all the things that went right and offer comments directed to specific people. Vague statements such as "we did a hell of a job with the marketing" are less helpful than telling the marketing team that the precision with which they created the marketing plan spelled the difference between success and failure.

What went wrong? A tougher subject, but one essential to address. Direct specific comments to individuals. If you pull punches during this phase, you will turn it into a meaningless exercise. Candid feedback is essential.

Next time. Use this opportunity to develop guidelines or ideas for working on similar projects.

This feedback process keeps teams working effectively. It enables a team to self-correct and increase its ability to function productively.

Here are some questions you might ask yourself as you prepare for giving feedback:

- What is the goal?
- What must the other person do to meet this goal?
- What is the person already doing that is helping meet this goal?
- What specific things must I tell this person? (specific action you want changed or improved, information about deadlines, etc.)
- What are the consequences to the unit if the person doesn't comply?
- When is the best time to talk with this person?
- Where should the meeting take place?

Appraisal is an expensive and unreliable way of getting quality. Checking and sorting and evaluating only sift what is done. What has to happen is prevention. The error that does not exist cannot be missed.

Philip Crosby
Quality Without Tears[3]

Feedback and the Road to Hell

Feedback is nothing more than information that allows people to monitor their progress. So why do so many leaders create their own hell by keeping people uninformed? Here are some of the most common reasons.

Fear. Fear may top the list. We fear their wrath, we fear hurting them, we fear the unknown, we fear making a mistake, we fear looking like a fool. That's a lot of fear.

Most of us are afraid to say something critical to another person and are embarrassed to say something nice (for fear that it will be taken the wrong way). That doesn't leave us much to say.

Although you might hope to overcome the fear of feedback encounters, you may always remain somewhat leery of them. So what? Feedback is a critical management tool and you must use it, no matter how you feel about it.

Too busy. Most managers are constantly busy, and one of the easiest things for them to forget about is ongoing feedback. We manage by exception, only looking at the things that go wrong, and then only after the problem has grown to disastrous proportions.

If we want performance to stay on track or improve, we must take the time to give information regarding performance to our staffs.

Lack of communication. Most of us assume that we are good, if not excellent, communicators — our directions are clear and concise, our critiques incisive, yet sensitive. The truth is that most managers give vague feedback, leaving everyone wondering what they had in mind. Remember, two-thirds of the people out there don't receive even adequate feedback. That means somebody's not giving it very well.

False assumptions. "If they need to know how they're doing, they'll ask." Most people are nervous about asking someone else for feedback — even someone as kind and open as you. And most people are nervous about talking to their bosses about performance. Aren't you?

The myth of performance reviews. Yearly performance reviews should not be confused with feedback. These formal meetings occur far too infrequently to be of much good in correcting or supporting activity. Think of it this way: there should be no surprises in a performance appraisal meeting. Feedback must be an ongoing activity.

As mentioned before, when people are worried about their reviews, they are less able to engage in healthy and candid dialogue regarding performance.

Style. Some give performance feedback in a way that is less than helpful. For example, Giuseppe Verdi was rehearsing for the important premiere of his opera *Aida*. Verdi struggled with the tenor, Giuseppe Fancelli, attempting to get him to sing a particular line correctly. "Having made Fancelli repeat the same phrase over and over without obtaining any result, Verdi rose to his feet, seized the tenor by the back of the neck, and while repeatedly pounding the man's forehead on the keyboard, burst out: 'When will anything ever get into your head? Never!'"[4] That's an example of poor style.

As a manager in a department store once told me, "It's the manager's job to help employees get outstanding ratings." In addition to supplying resources, it is a manager's responsibility to provide staff with information regarding performance. Think of the people who report to you as your customers. What do they need from you in order to make you look brilliant?

12

Supporting Your People

What I say about Norton is one thing; what I feel about him is another.

— Ralph Kramden (Jackie Gleason)
"The Honeymooners"

The Maurer Theory of Human Development implies that we are all nine-year-old children trapped in the bodies of adults. Nine-year-olds want to know how they are doing — do Mommy and Daddy really care? Nine-year-olds need support and encouragement. As respectable card-carrying adults, we would never think of asking our boss what he or she thought of us. We would never ask if the boss liked our work. Nevertheless, we need to hear those supportive words, and for most, those words come infrequently.

People hardly receive adequate information on job performance, let alone hear something as soft as supportive words. There is a difference between performance feedback and support. Although performance feedback — information regarding how well we are working to standards — certainly can be supportive, it is a different sort of information. When you run the tutorial for new software, error messages and suggestions appear telling you what you did right and wrong and making suggestions for corrective actions — information that is clear performance feedback.

However, when you do it right, a hand never reaches out from the screen to pat you on the back or offer to buy you a beer — now that would be support.

The bumper sticker reading "Have you hugged your kid today?" was popular a few years back. Presumably, it was meant to remind people to be kind to their children. If we must be reminded that it is a good practice to be nice to those we love, how big does the bumper sticker need to be that tells us to do the same when the relationship is a bit more tenuous?

Recognition at the Corporate Level

Often organizations offer a variety of options for recognizing achievement. You should use these options and, if necessary, learn how to cut paperwork to reward people quickly.

Bonuses. People love money. A bonus tied directly to outstanding performance is rewarding and offers tangible thanks. Some organizations ruin an otherwise good bonus system by requiring managers to jump through hoop after hoop, sign multiple forms, and wait for a special committee to grant approval. Six months later the employee receives the reward. Better late than never, but not by much. If the organization allows you to give bonuses, find a way to get the money into people's hands quickly.

Award dinners. People in many organizations look forward to the recognition dinner or similar event. These work when the award ceremony is sincerely felt and awards are given fairly throughout the organization.

Profit sharing. Profit or gain sharing is growing in popularity as a way of rewarding people. In 1989 negotiations with all three American car manufacturers, the United Auto Workers tied part of their compensation to productivity. It makes sense. Healthy partnerships cannot be created when one side reaps most of the benefits. Although ESOPs (employee stock ownership plans) and profit sharing are out of the hands of most midlevel managers, they are worth encouraging if your company starts considering them.

Gifts. Bausch and Lomb gives managers a list of possible gifts and rewards they can offer employees. No paperwork, no delays. The manager is free to choose anything from a small gift certificate to a cash award. (Larger cash awards must go through an approval process.) Managers in other organizations are encouraged to create their own rewards — dinners, flowers, even clambakes. The company simply provides the funds.

Trips. Some larger companies give trips to top achievers. Often these trips are so exciting and so "first-class" that people talk about them for years. However, individual awards should be given only to those who are generally recognized as top performers.

Corporate Recognition and the Road to Hell

Even something as seemingly positive as corporate recognition and awards can have negative repercussions. Consider these hazards.

Silly or demeaning rewards. In *The Bank Dick*, W.C. Fields risks his life to capture a gang of robbers, and returns the stolen money to the bank. His reward: a hearty handshake from the bank president and a calendar titled "Springtime in Lompoc."

One employee at an auto plant received a lighter after making a significant time-saving suggestion. He quit making suggestions. An "employee of the month" award covered with grease, tucked away in the corner of some employee cafeteria, quickly loses its significance.

One person's reward is another's punishment. An awards banquet may make some feel great and embarrass others. Rewards and recognition must be viewed as rewarding to the receiver, not to the giver. Regarding the certificates his company gave to field sales staff who work out of their cars, one district sales manager asked, "Where are they going to hang the damn things?"

A cheap date. Nonmonetary rewards are given in an effort to keep costs low. Instead of sharing in the profits brought by higher quality and service, management finds small, insignificant, and inexpensive ways of rewarding people. One manager told me that his staff was getting tired of the little thank-you tokens he was giving them; he wanted to know what he could do next. He should have realized that his employees weren't pack rats who delighted in going from one shiny object to another.

Unfair rewards. Sometimes, one person is singled out for recognition while other highly productive members of the team stand on the sidelines. This is especially unfair when the reward translates into dollars — raises, bonuses, trips. Make sure that others aren't left behind yelling "bon voyage" through gritted teeth.

Pro forma. Some recognition programs are so old and tired that no one could possibly get excited about them. Often the awards are so diluted that everyone goes home a winner. Sometimes the simple act of showing up is cause enough for a certificate and a handshake from the boss. These awards are jokes — don't use them.

What Managers Can Do

The key is doing it. Just do it; the technique will follow. Just as individuals differ in what they find reassuring and supportive, so managers differ in what techniques work for them. Here are some that many managers have found effective.

Sharing the victory. Talk up your staff to others. Give credit to those who do the work. This is supportive and may help their career development.

Saying "thank you." Think of special ways of saying "thank you." Flowers are special for some. One manager sends thank-you cards. This means a real greeting or note card, not a memo. Another manager gave members of his staff tickets for a million-dollar lottery in thanks for a job well done. It cost him only a few dollars, but the gifts were warmly received. Another manager draws smiley faces on service reports he likes. (Although cute little smiley faces make me retch, they were appreciated by the person who received them.)

If it weren't for the people, all we'd be is a bunch of drafting tables.

— Partner in architectural firm

Roving award. A large nonprofit agency uses an excellence award that moves from department to department. The trophy stays in one office for a while, then travels when another significant event occurs.

Letters of recognition. A letter is sent to the CEO with courtesy copies to the employee and to his or her file. Obviously, a letter sent just to the employee's file hardly provides recognition.

The U.S. Postal Service has a policy stating that any letters of recommendation coming from outside the service must be taken out of personnel files after one year, whereas official letters from managers and staff remain in the files indefinitely. One manager handles this policy by formally acknowledging the letters his staff receives and guaranteeing that memory of the good words will live.

Pool of $. Some managers set aside part of the annual budget to create a pool to use for bonuses. This allows the leader to give a reward without sending a request through what could be a lengthy approval process. Although these funds can be used for cash bonuses, other options include:

- Small gifts. One manager gives flowers or a restaurant gift certificate to people who do something special, or as special thanks to people who routinely do good work.
- Beer busts. Or an afternoon tea if you prefer. Stop work early on Friday and send out for pizza as a way of thanking the staff for working hard during the last quarter.

What If No Money Is Available?

Please don't skip down to this section hoping to find cheap ways to thank people. If your organization is making money or working more productively because of your hard-working staff, your people deserve to share in the gain.

Ask. A manager in a government agency asked his staff, "What non-monetary rewards would you like?" They knew that his ability to give monetary rewards was limited. Their response to his question surprised him — he heard ideas that would never have occurred to him. People wanted time to attend conferences, greater use of flextime, opportunities to work on particular projects, and so forth.

Too often managers wring their hands trying to think of some way to recognize achievement when the answer lies right in front of them — they simply need to ask.

Simply say "Thanks." A radical notion, I admit, but a simple acknowledgment of your appreciation that an employee stayed late to finish a report or covered for you in a meeting is important.

Make support a standard. One nonprofit membership organization considered making support of its volunteers an operating standard. Elevating recognition to the level of an operating standard may seem excessive, but members felt that appreciation was often overlooked and that keeping good volunteers was vital to the organization's survival.

Give time off. Look the other way. Allow someone to take off the afternoon or to take a long weekend without applying for annual leave. Don't worry about how it will look, just do it.

Positive feedback meeting. Organizational development consultant David Coleman introduced me to the following technique. It's simple and effective.

1. Ask each member of the group to write his or her name on top of a blank sheet of paper and pass it to the person to the left.
2. Each person must write one sentence about this person that begins, "I appreciate . . .," "I admire . . .," or perhaps "I respect . . . ." For example, one person may write, "I appreciate your willingness to stay until the job gets done."
3. Pass each sheet to the left once again and write a sentence on the new sheet.
4. Continue this process until everyone has his or her own sheet back again.
5. One person volunteers to pass his or her sheet around for oral comments. As it makes the rounds, each person reads the sentence he or she wrote and expands on the sentence. For instance, "I wrote, 'I appreciate your willingness to stay until the job is done.' Often during the past few months you have stayed here well beyond closing time to make sure everything was ready to go out the next morning. That saved me a lot of hassles. So, thanks." Others may add to this oral comment. Then continue passing the sheet around so that everyone is able to read and comment on the sentence he or she wrote.
6. Repeat the process so that everyone's written comments are read aloud.

The feedback recipient has a very simple job during this session — shut up and listen. So often we talk away positive feedback — making excuses, giving credit to someone else, or telling the feedback-giver why he or she is wrong.

Personal Recognition and the Road to Hell

On the personal level, there are also pitfalls to avoid in recognizing achievements of your employees.

The wake phenomenon. Poor Harry is dead and we stand around telling tales about our lost friend — about all the wonderful things he did for us. Of course, we never told Harry this while he was alive, and he may have some difficulty hearing us now. Don't wait — let people know how you feel.

The boss claims all the glory. One manager planned and executed a project successfully. When the project won an award, both the project manager and her boss attended the awards celebration. But the boss, who had only minor involvement in the project, sat at the speaker's table, accepted the award, and never mentioned the work of her staff member. The project manager watched from the back of the hall. She has since found another job.

They already know. We often assume that people who look strong and secure don't need our support and encouragement, but they do. Once Sir Alec Guinness was on location shooting a film. The cast and crew, who were in awe of this great actor, gave him wide berth. Each day he withdrew more and more into himself between takes. Finally, the director went to his trailer and asked if anything was wrong. Guinness looked up and asked, "Is my acting all right?" The director replied that, of course, he was doing all right. He was Alec Guinness, he was doing wonderfully; surely he knew that. Guinness told him that he had to understand actors: that although they may be adult in many areas of their lives, when it comes to acting they are vulnerable little children who can never mature — and who need all the support and attention they can get.

Phony gestures. Offering support because you read it here or because it seems like a good gimmick will not work. We all see through phonies.

Embarrassing the recipient. The support should fit the person. Some people hate to be singled out publicly and dread being asked to stand and take a bow.

Unfair recognition. One person is singled out for praise while the others who worked equally hard and well get no thanks.

Confusing smiles for money. This chapter looks at day-to-day support. As essential as this type of support is, you should never confuse it with the necessity of paying people well.

It is far too easy to take recognition for granted and overlook its importance. Managers must reward and support people for two good reasons: it encourages people to continue meeting goals, and it is the right thing to do. As Robert Waterman suggests, "Treat people right. It can't hurt."

13

Encouraging Initiative

Success is the ability to go from failure to failure with great enthusiasm.

Winston Churchill

People must be encouraged to take risks — to try new approaches, make off-the-wall suggestions, use their own initiative when faced with problems. Without support and encouragement, few will remain active problem-solvers.

Many organizations impose silly requirements on staff. You may recall the example of the cafeteria attendant who was reprimanded for serving toast at noon. It seems unlikely that this employee will go out of his way again to do something special for a customer. His organization fails on two counts — it places guidelines over service, and it encourages management practices that sap initiative. If you give employees too many "toast-at-noon" restrictions, they will learn quickly that it would be foolish to try anything new. Work soon becomes "just a job."

Most employees will play by the rules you create no matter how stupid they are. You should help them challenge bureaucratic toast-at-noon rules. When people see a problem, they must be free to act. They must know that they will be supported for taking a chance. Here are some things to consider.

117

What It Takes

Making a Clear Policy. The one-page Nordstrom employee handbook simply advises staff to use their best judgment at all times. People on the sales floor know that they are there to serve customers. Managers work the floor and watch new salespeople in action. They advise and coach employees on alternatives they might consider when working with customers. But most important, they allow people to do their jobs hassle-free.

Results? Why, man, I have gotten a lot of results. I know several thousand things that won't work.

— Thomas Edison

Some employees go to amazing lengths to serve their customers. Once a man came into a clothing store looking for a particular jacket. Although the store didn't have it in his size, the salesman knew that a nearby competitor carried the same item. He called the competitor and asked if they would honor his store's price, which was a few dollars less, if he sent this customer over. The competitor refused. (Even though the competitor was going to be given a customer, they didn't want to lose the few dollars. Must have been company policy.) The salesman went to the competitor, purchased the coat at retail price, returned, and sold it to his customer for the lower price. No policy manual or training told him to handle the situation in that manner; he simply used his best judgment. Past experience had taught him that such actions would be applauded.

Priming the pump. The history of work in America is not brimming with tales of individuals within organizations taking chances. We celebrate the lone inventors, of course, but not the potential inventors within organizations. We must show people that it is necessary for them to take initiative. Saying "use your best judgment" or placing that phrase in a memo one time will not change the great suspicion most have toward taking risks.

Look for opportunities to encourage initiative. One manager often responds to new ideas with, "We've never tried that before. Let's see what we can learn from it." He approaches it as an opportunity to learn more about what works and what does not. Knowing that an idea is an opportunity to learn something eliminates the pressure of perfection.

A marketing group within one large corporation holds a retreat in order to demonstrate to its annual crop of new MBAs that they encourage risk taking. The leaders tell stories of championing products that never made it to grocery shelves but did create real opportunities for the company to learn more about product development and the market. These professionals were living testimonials that risks gone bad did not signal the end of a career.

Go ahead and do it; you can always apologize later.

— Grace Hopper
Rear Admiral, U.S. Navy

Handling Failure

The test of a "use your best judgment" policy is when someone does take a chance and it fails miserably and the world doesn't end. One time an employee entered the office of Thomas Watson, Sr., the founder of IBM, hat in hand. The employee had just made a mistake that had cost the company millions. "Sir, I imagine you'd like my resignation?" he asked.

"What, are you kidding?" Watson replied. "I just spent 10 million dollars on your education."[1]

Watson was no fool. He didn't encourage cavalier risks, but when someone had the guts to back a well-considered idea that failed, Watson demonstrated that he valued initiative over safety.

One corporate vice president advertises his own failures. He wants people to see that it is all right to fail, and that everyone can learn from the mistakes — and the successes — of others. He creates a climate that says failures are opportunities to learn if we pay attention to them.

Risk and the Road to Hell

If you're going to encourage reasoned risk, you have to really do it, and be prepared to live with the consequences.

"But it's our policy." We are so afraid of something going wrong that we guard against every contingency by creating rules and guidelines for every activity.

"Take a chance, but don't you dare fail." If high-wire artists took that advice, we'd see Not-So-Amazing Wallendas perform their feats on a rope stretched across the floor of the circus tent.

I recall a successful entrepreneur who had given himself this good advice: "Whenever I am faced with an important decision, I try to make a decision that could either get me promoted or fired. I have no patience for safe bureaucratic decisions."

By letting his men play naturally and relaxed, (Duke) Ellington is able to probe the intimate recesses of their minds and find things that not even the musicians thought were there.

— Billy Strayhorn

14

Helping Employees Develop

I've learned from my mistakes. I'm sure that I could repeat them exactly.

— Peter Cook
from the "Frog and Peach" routine

Delegating authority to others is risky. They could let you down — miss deadlines, turn in shoddy work, or forget about the assignments. The excuses for not handing over authority to others could fill this book. But if you want to increase commitment to quality and service, you must give control to the people on your staff. They must be the first to demand high quality and they must be the ones who go the extra mile to make a customer happy. Without their help you will die young.

People who take risks and succeed are people who know what they are doing. Karl Wallenda, the great aerialist, didn't start off high above the big top. He started close to the ground and used a net. When you are learning, it is perfectly all right to be a Not-So-Amazing-Wallenda. Only a fool would imagine he could walk across a stretched rope 50 feet above the ground on the first try. Only fools delegate without determining how much can be delegated and how soon.

The question is, development to what end? In the best of all possible work units, employees anticipate problems and opportunities, and take action to improve the organization. Your goal might be to give maximum control to the people closest to the work. To do that you must determine what "maximum control" means and how to get there. You need a plan to help people learn the skills they need to become masters of their craft.

The Stages of Development

There are skills we must learn in order to perform a job well, whether the job is tightrope walking, pizza making, or machine tooling. The manager's job is to help the employee or team learn the essential skills.

Your help may come in many forms, from simply pointing the way to suggesting a complex training program, but first you must understand the stages of development.

Stage One: Orientation. Stage One is for people new to the organization or the department. It is the grand tour. Help them see the big picture; introduce them to all the players and explain their respective roles in the unit. Let them see how the work is done and how decisions are made. Introduce them to suppliers and customers. Show them samples of the product or the type of work you expect.

It is surprising how often a new employee is greeted, shown a desk, and then forgotten. The new organization is still a vast uncharted wilderness to these people; you must provide a map and a guide.

A person in Stage One may be someone recently hired who knows little about the work or someone who has been given a dramatically new assignment. The employee who leaves work on Friday as a self-respecting engineer and returns on Monday bearing the title of manager is in Stage One. It is obvious that a new recruit with no experience needs direction and support, but the need is not so obvious in the case of an engineer who has been around for ten years. The skills of engineering are wildly different from the skills of leading people; this person will have much to learn. The faulty assumption that plagues too many organizations is that a good technician will somehow magically become a good manager overnight.

Also place in Stage One someone who is expanding the boundaries of his or her current job. For example, an hourly employee who, in addition to his or her regular duties of working on the line, will begin taking part in problem-solving meetings, needs help learning this new set of skills.

Some general guidelines for Stage One follow.

Provide clear and specific direction. Begin with the development goal. Encourage questions. Either work with the employee to map out the development plan or suggest a plan that has worked for others. For example, say your experience has shown that rotational assignments help new employees learn how business is conducted more quickly than any other method. Describe the assignments and ask for questions.

Remember the little things. Once we've worked somewhere for a while, we take much for granted. Everything from knowing the idiosyncrasies of the photocopy machine to knowing where supplies are kept becomes second nature. Minifrustrations add to the potential bewilderment of new employees.

Offer lots of support. New employees usually need lots of encouragement. They won't ask for it, but most wonder how they are doing. Your support makes it easier for them to feel like they are part of the unit. If you want partnership, you must make sure people feel like partners.

Play Carnac. Remember the last time you changed positions or organizations? Those first few days were filled with unasked questions. Try to be like Johnny Carson's Great Carnac character and answer questions like the following before they are asked.

- Will I fit in here?
- Can I cut it?

- How am I doing?
- What am I expected to do?
- What are the quality and service standards?
- What resources can I use?
- How can I get help when I have questions?
- Who are the other players and what are their roles?
- Who are our customers and suppliers? What do they expect from me?
- What are the rules here?

Make it easy for the employee to ask questions and admit mistakes.

Work with a master. Allow the new employee to work with a master, someone who can do the job extremely well. Watching a master at work can do more than all the books or training courses in helping someone see how to do the job.

Treat the new people like you wish you had been treated when you were new.

Stage Two: Apprenticeship. Once the employee learns the basics, responsibility should be increased gradually. Look for a balance between risk and safety; offer enough risk to create challenges and encourage learning, and enough safety to keep failures small. While we learn from both successes and failures, major failures may work against development. The employee may begin playing it safe to avoid another error.

Provide direction. Obviously the employee still needs guidance, but you should look for opportunities to begin collaborating so that she can learn from experience. Giving up control is difficult for many managers, but it is an essential skill if you want people to take on more responsibility.

Offer support. Encourage people to take more risks by attempting new tasks, making higher-level decisions, and taking initiative. Make failures acceptable by treating them as learning experiences.

Clarify expectations. Make certain the employee understands what you expect. For example, you might tell the new employee that you want him or her to be able to handle all requests for information from customers within three months, and that eventually you hope to delegate that task completely to him or her.

Create a development plan. Work with the new employee to create a development plan that may include developmental assignments, meetings with key players, visits to other locations, and training.

Give feedback. Make certain the employee receives all the feedback he or she needs to stay on track. Make it easy for him or her to come to you and ask questions or get advice. If you create a partnership with the apprentice, then you both bear equal responsibility for making certain he or she stays informed.

Reward. Make certain you reward and recognize actions that are consistent with your unit's values and vision.

Stage Three: Mastery. Once the development goal has been accomplished, you should consider ways to keep learning fresh. Conditions change: We get rusty; we need reminders. Training, conferences, meetings, books, and visits to other locations can all help keep people up-to-date and keep thinking crisp.

Watch for stagnation at the mastery level. Most people thrive on at least some degree of challenge. Once we get too good at something or too comfortable, we begin to fidget and look around for something else. Development never ends. The manager and employee need to find creative ways to keep work fresh and alive.

To begin the development process, you will need to identify a developmental goal, assess the current situation, and create a development plan.

Consider working in partnership with the employee or work team to create a developmental goal and plan. This collaboration frees you from pretending to be an all-knowing seer. It's their work unit, too; let them take responsibility with you in making it work.

> *One boss I had, his philosophy was whatever a person*
> *thinks he can do or has shown he can do, have him do 10 to 20*
> *percent more than that.*
> — Employee in an aerospace company

Identifying the Development Goal

Development should be toward a goal. A developmental goal might read:

- The work team will eventually take over major responsibility for finding ways to improve quality on the factory floor.
- The executive assistant will take over full editorial responsibility for the monthly newsletter to members: solicit and edit articles and supervise publication and distribution.
- The customer representative will handle all complaints creatively and to the satisfaction of the customer and the company.

The goal is the foundation; it directs all development activities. The goal allows you and the employee or team to identify what stands between them and the goal. Once you have established this goal and assessed the current level of development with regard to key tasks, creating a development plan is relatively easy.

Staff Development Profile

This short assessment allows you to determine the readiness of your employees to take on more responsibility. This is not a personality test, nor is it a total rating of a person's skills. It is merely a "snapshot" that allows you to assess their readiness to take on particular responsibilities.

Employee's Name _____ Date _____

Identify specific area of responsibility (such as sales, developing a new program, operating a sophisticated milling machine, etc.).

_____

_____

To the extent possible, rate the employee on factors related to the area of responsibility listed above.

Independence

Rate each item on a scale from 1 to 5. 1 = never, none, or unlike this individual; 5 – always, a lot, very much like this individual.

___ Likes to work with little or no supervision.
___ Takes initiative to solve problems.
___ Knows when to ask for help
___ Works well with colleagues.
___ Takes initiative to go beyond what is assigned.

Skills

Indicate which of the following best describes the person's skills to handle this job.

1. Could take on full authority for this particular task today.
2. With minimal training, coaching, or discussion could take on this assignment.
3. With significant training or coaching, could probably take on this assignment.
4. This person could never take over full authority for this assignment.
5. Insufficient information to assess skill level.

Commitment

Assess this employee using a 1 to 5 scale (1 is low; 5 is high).

___ This person meets high standards or sets high standards for his or her own work.
___ This person does whatever it takes to get the job done.

Interpretation

Independence

A high score (20 to 25) indicates the person probably shows sufficient skills to work well on an assignment with little supervision.

Lower scores (1 to 19) indicate that the person may need to be given more independence incrementally. Think of teaching a child to ride a bicycle. You hold tight when the child first gets on the bike and then gradually loosen your grip as you offer suggestions to the rider. Adults often need the same gradual letting-go.

The lower the score, the more help you will need to offer.

Skills

If anyone scored a "5," you might wonder why you aren't taking advantage of this person's skills already; "4" indicates someone who is almost ready to take on the assignment. Consider discussing your expectations with him or her to find out what he or she thinks is needed. This should be an easy task. "3" and "2" require a development plan. "1" is tricky. The person may lack skills or may never have been given an opportunity. As hard as it may be, I encourage you to create a development plan for this person. If you are successful and the person is able to take on even a little more responsibility, you are better off than if you had assumed the person could never do the job.

Commitment

A score of 8 to 10 is a joy to behold. Get out of the way and let these people do their jobs. Scores of 5 to 7 may simply indicate that you need to define the tasks, the importance of the work, and the importance of their participation in this project.

Lower scores (1 to 4) may indicate a serious problem, but assume the best — that given increased responsibility and authority, this person will rise to the challenge. Give increased responsibility in doses that you can stand. Perhaps you might delegate a portion of a task and observe how the employee handles it. If that works, loosen the reins. If increased responsibility doesn't work, look to yourself once again. Ask, "Is there any way in which I might be contributing to the problem?" If you are certain the answer is no, then consider patience, prayer, or personnel action.

If both you and the employee filled out the assessment, discuss any differences in scores. Whenever the employee scores himself higher in a category, give him the benefit of the doubt. Say he rates himself high on commitment, and you rate him low. Acknowledge the difference and discuss the reasons for the disparity, and then offer to treat him as if commitment were high. By all means, express your reservations, but give him an opportunity to demonstrate his commitment.

Commitment, skill, or independence may be low, or it may seem low simply because the employee has never been given an opportunity to use these skills. Be willing to challenge your own assumptions about the other person. Often the challenge of increased authority surprises even the employee.

If the assessment raised more questions than it answered, then you must continue the assessment process. You must find answers to all your questions. To involve others sensibly, you must base your decision on real, rather than hoped-for, information.

A sound assessment is the foundation for a good development plan.

The Development Plan

Work closely with the employee or team to create a development plan. This collaboration could save countless hours, dollars, and frustration.

Allow the employee to work with you in identifying learning opportunities. If you expect a first-line supervisor to apply the principles of effective teamwork, does it make a difference where or how she learns these skills? If she says she can handle the challenge of working with a team, without training, trust her. If she fails, then consider an alternative.

The development plan needn't be a formal document. You simply need to address the questions, "Where do you want to go?" and "How are you going to get there?" The sample plan that appears later in this chapter allows for a great deal of latitude in preparing a plan. (A blank copy is included in Appendix B.) The plan includes:

A Goal. This is the development goal discussed earlier. Set a target for reaching this goal. A goal may be focused on a particular set of tasks such as "learning facilitator skills in order to conduct quality circle meetings successfully," or it may be a more complex and longer-range goal such as "As branch manager, this employee will be able to lead all activities within the branch such as developing marketing plans, coordinating activities of staff, hiring, budgeting, and so forth."

An Explanation. This is the rationale and explains why the development goal is important, helping new employees see why you and your staff made the decisions you did. It explains the method behind the madness.

Stage One (Orientation). Explain how you will introduce the person to the new procedures, people, and so forth. Identify initial learning opportunities such as training, rotational assignments, or pairing the person with someone with more experience.

Stage Two (Apprenticeship). This stage may include advanced training, but its primary emphasis is on giving the employee ways to practice the skills without excessive risk. Identify those opportunities.

Stage Three (Mastery). The employee knows the skills and is practicing them. Since development should be constant, identify the developmental activities he or she will need in order to continue working effectively toward the goals.

- What assistance do I anticipate I will need? The employee describes those areas where he or she anticipates extra support or guidance may be needed. He or she might request an open-door policy with a particular staff member so that critical questions can be answered in a timely fashion.
- Resources (books, coaches, other training, other units, etc.). These resources may never be used, but brainstorming during the planning phase shows the richness or paucity of help available. For example, a branch chief who is learning the skills of leading a self-managed team may find comfort in knowing others who have made the same journey — that if he or she ever feels in a bind, there is someone to call.

Does everyone need a plan? What about the person who could be given more responsibility tomorrow — no training, no coaching, he doesn't need a thing. The answer should be obvious.

Sit down with this person and tell him what you propose — that is, to give him more authority. Explain what you have in mind; discuss it with him. Then give him the assignment. Period. Count your blessings. (Refer to Chapter 10 for suggestions on how to delegate.)

The Heart of the Plan

One government manager refers to "expanding the comfort zone" when she talks about helping others develop skills. She believes that people are willing to take risks and try new challenges if they know that they are still working within a safe range. Although the task might be new and risky, the employee is able to apply his or her experience from other assignments and experiences.

> *I wanted the music this new group would play to be freer . . . . See, if you put a musician in a place where he has to do something different from what he does all the time, then he can do that — but he's got to think differently to do it. He has to use his imagination, be more creative, more innovative; he's got to take more risks. He's got to play above what he knows — far above it. . . . [He] will expect things differently, will anticipate and know something different is coming down. I've always told the musicians in my band to play what they know and then play above that. Because then anything can happen, and that's where great art and music happen.*
>
> — Miles Davis
> *Miles*[1]

Consider the following options as you create a development plan with your staff. Some learn best by attending workshops, others by reading, others by osmosis — some pick up a little here and a little there. This is why collaborating with the employee is so important. Your staff has been suffering under an unresponsive educational system all their lives. They know what they *don't* want — give them a chance to invent a program that works. The best teachers know that when people are given the opportunity to create their own plan for learning, their commitment to learning rises considerably.

We spend too much on training that misses the mark. How many organizations send all managers to the same training courses, requiring them to jump through prescribed hoops on their way up the corporate ladder? I recall a cartoon that pictured the educational system as prying open a head, filling it with sand, sealing it once again, then placing the graduate's mortarboard on top. Too much is wasted in pouring sand of equal doses into everyone's heads.

Use training wisely. Carefully consider which courses are essential, which rotational assignments make sense, which on-the-job projects truly move the person closer to the performance goal. Recently I worked with a ranking executive who had been through exactly the same five-day management development course twice, but the second time it was as an official part of his development plan. This is hardly a good use of talent, money, or time. Isn't it better to give people responsibility for determining when and how they will develop skills?

OJT. On-the-job training. Nordstrom doesn't send new salespeople off to formal training programs; they put new employees on the floor with experienced sales associates. This gives them an opportunity to see how the job is done correctly, to ask questions, and to see how masters solve problems.

Although OJT is often overlooked, it can be a powerful way to learn. The Center for Creative Leadership found that many people who rose far in their organizations were people who, early in their careers, worked for someone who was very good at his or her job. In other words, they saw the job done right. They saw what was possible.

On May 6, 1954, Roger Bannister ran the mile in three minutes 59.4 seconds. He was the first man to break the four-minute mile barrier. Within a year, 37 others ran the mile in under four minutes. Within two years, 300 more had broken that "impossible" barrier. During this time, human physiology did not take some giant evolutionary leap as a result of Bannister's accomplishment. Instead, a new standard had been set: people saw that it was possible to run the mile in under four minutes.

People who never see someone handle a customer complaint well or solve a problem under pressure lack a model of what is possible. Consider matching people who need to improve a skill with someone who has mastered it.

Sit in on meetings. Give people an opportunity to see how decisions get made — what thinking goes into critical decisions, how resources are allocated, the problems that are faced.

Explain how you work. Allow the employee to follow you around and ask questions.

Create an internship. An internship allows the employee to be a student on the job. The internship could be in another department, another organization, or on your own shop floor. What distinguishes this assignment from others is that the individual is given permission to be a learner. Time is set aside for the employee to ask questions; the "student" isn't expected to be a star. An internship gives the employee the freedom to make mistakes.

Collaborate on decision making. Bring the employee in on important decisions — not to observe, but to make the decisions with you.

Have the old teach the new. Procter and Gamble, to develop new managers, sometimes keeps the old manager on for up to six months to help the new manager learn the skills needed to do the job.

Assign a sponsor. The U.S. Army often assigns sponsors to soldiers who are new to a base. The sponsor is there to help the soldier learn the ropes — how to do things from finding suitable living arrangements to learning how decisions are made on base.

Rate yourself. Make development a measurable item on your performance plan. Show your commitment to helping people gain the skills they need by basing part of your performance on their success.

Training. Training is last on this list because formal training should be the last thing you consider. Training is expensive and often takes people away from the job. I happen to be a big fan of training when it is used as part of an intelligently designed plan to increase skills, but too often it is hoped that training will achieve the miracle of Lourdes. Send them off to training for the cure and be absolved of responsibility.

If you are going to use training, be certain that the training course you send employees to or the one you ask to have designed for you truly meets the goals you have set. Demand something for your money.

> *You can never learn anything unless you are willing to take a risk and tolerate a little randomness in your life.*
>
> — Heinz Pagels
> *Dreams of Reason?*

Development and the Road to Hell

Staff development is a critical aspect of managing. Watch for these areas that can create difficulty.

Training for training's sake. People go to training for the damned-est reasons. Some organizations send people to high-priced courses as a reward, others send people as a punishment: Harry's a bad communicator — send him to training for the cure. St. Bernadette wasn't a human resources professional; miracles seldom occur at training seminars.

Training is seen as the magic solution to all our problems; however, you should determine whether training is truly the right solution. Robert Mager uses this simple test. He asks: If you held a gun to their heads, could they do it? If the answer is "yes," then lack of training isn't the problem. Spend your money wisely.

Past performance. Forget about the past. Use the information in front of you. If the person lacks the skills to do the job, do something so that he can learn those skills. If he lacks commitment, give him another chance. Give him the opportunity to redeem himself. I am not suggesting that you close your eyes and give a major assignment to someone who has not shown he is capable of doing it. I am suggesting that you start building. Often the people who are labeled "sleepers" or "troublemakers" have been in that role for so long that even they fail to see the possibilities.

Infrequent feedback. Without regular guidance and critique, the employee is left to flounder.

Assuming too much. Organizations often assume that simply because someone was a terrific accountant, lawyer, or engineer, she will be a marvelous team leader, manager, whatever. So without any training, coaching, or OJT, the new manager is flung into battle and expected to succeed. When she fails, we shake our heads and acknowledge Lawrence Peter's admonition that people rise to their level of incompetence.

Although the development plan described in this chapter is designed to increase a person's skills related to a particular set of tasks, it does not preclude the possibility or necessity of working on career development plans that prepare people for their next position in the organization. This plan is simply a way to help your unit ensure that everyone has the skills and experience to meet the highest possible standards.

An Employee Development Plan

Ideally, the manager and employee or work team should be partners in the creation of this plan. The employee probably knows where he or she is deficient, how he or she learns best (workshops? on-the-job-training? reading?) and how long it might take to gain mastery.

GOAL _____

ESTIMATED TIME FOR COMPLETION _____

EXPLANATION _____

_____

_____

STAGE ONE (Orientation):

STAGE TWO (Apprenticeship):

STAGE THREE (Mastery):

What assistance do I anticipate I will need? (To be filled out by employee.)

_____

_____

_____

Resources (books, coaches, training, other units, etc.):

_____

_____

_____

15

Building an Effective Team

*If you put a production fellow and a maintenance fellow
and an engineer together, you're going to find out pretty quickly
whether something has a chance of getting off the ground. And if
it does, having them there means that you have a pretty good
chance of getting it up and working.*

— Gordon E. Forward
Harvard Business Review[1]

Like it or not, managers must work with teams. The new work
unit is often arranged around a team concept. Ad hoc committees
form to solve immediate problems, staff meetings inform people of
current activity and serve as a forum for ideas, and interdepartmental teams work on long-range projects.

Well-run teams accomplish more than a collection of individuals could. Teams can harness resources, share information, pro-
voke, counsel, and pitch in to help members during crises. But
many teams fall short of this potential by being fractious and ill-
informed. They waste the time and energy of the members.

Reprinted by permission of *Harvard Business Review*. An excerpt from
"Wide-open management at Chapparal Steel," Gordon E. Forward, inter-
viewed by Alan M. Kantrow (May/June 1986). Copyright © 1989 by the
President and Fellows of Harvard College; all rights reserved.

Occasionally a group of individuals meets and everything seems to click, right from the beginning. The team works productively and people actually like being around each other. Most teams are not dreams to behold, however. They require effort to make them work well.

This chapter covers some of the tools you need to organize and maintain a productive team. The tools are not magic formulas. They will not necessarily make you fall in love with the other members, but if they are applied diligently, they will help you make sure that the work done by the team is well-considered and effectively executed.

Diagnostic Check for Teams

New and existing teams need criteria by which they can examine working practices and make needed adjustments. Use the following list to assess any given team's ability to function productively. A poor rating in any of the categories is a signal that you should take some corrective action.

Mission/Goals

Write a short description (25 words or less) of the team's major responsibilities (its reason for being). You might limit the statement to a particular project, addressing the purpose of the project.

_____

_____

_____

_____

_____

Roles and Responsibilities

Define your major roles in this team (scribe, team leader, liaison to suppliers, etc.),

_____

_____

_____

Define the roles of the other members of the team.

_____

_____

_____

Coordination with Other Teams

Do we actively coordinate our work with the work of our customers and suppliers? Give examples.

_____

_____

_____

Approach

Describe how the team analyzes problems and makes decisions.

_____

_____

_____

Day-to-Day Work

Identify an incident that exemplifies the way in which the team works together day in and day out.

_____

_____

_____

Quality of the Relationships

Respond to each of the following:

• Is it fun working on this team? In what ways?

_____

_____

_____

• Do I feel others listen to me? Do I listen to others? Explain.

_____

_____

_____

• Do I openly encourage others and delight in the successes of team members? In what ways?

_____

_____

_____

• Do we share resources with each other? Describe.

_____

_____

_____

• Do we pitch in to help each other? Give an example.

_____

_____

_____

Interpreting the Assessment

Mission/Goals

The team should know why it exists. All team members should be able to define the mission of the team and state the goals of current projects. In other words, all members of the team should share a common understanding of why they are together and what they are supposed to accomplish.

Too often teams suffer from diffuse or vague goals. Not surprisingly, the work of these teams is inconsistent. One person's top priority item is another's low-priority item simply because they lack a common understanding of the team's direction.

Even slight variations in responses indicate that priorities could be quite diverse. Think of sighting a rifle. An error of mere hundredths of an inch on the sight will cause the bullet to travel far off course.

Roles and Responsibilities

All members of a team must know their respective roles. No basketball coach would ever build a team without identifying forwards, guards, and center, or without being certain that all players know precisely what they are supposed to do on the court.

Roles are not job descriptions. Roles are functional day-to-day "whom should I pass to?" responsibilities. Who is project manager? Who handles budget? Who will coordinate with the office down the hall?

Clear roles and responsibilities increase the chances that people will know what they are supposed to do. Less will fall through the cracks, duplication of effort will be reduced, and turf battles will be diminished.

Coordination with Other Teams

All teams have suppliers and customers. Teams must understand their relationship with other individuals and units. Who must complete work before we can begin? Whom do we serve? Work must be coordinated with these other individuals and teams.

Understanding these relationships helps team members know where to create links with other units to speed up delivery of items or to ensure that the customer will be satisfied with the team's product or service. Teams must make sure that natural boundaries don't become fortresses that exclude others. When the boundary becomes a fortress, suppliers are transformed into "those damn suppliers" who never get things to us on time, and customers turn into "those jerks who are never satisfied with anything."

Approach

Teams must determine how they will address problems: What approaches will they take in analyzing the causes of a problem, and what steps will they take in determining solutions? How will the team make decisions — by committee, by executive fiat, by the loudest and last to speak, or by a more democratic process?

New teams should create operating norms that guide their actions. Norms or procedures may change, but at least they change by plan rather than by chance. The team might agree to a norm that all meetings start and end on time, or to making sure all team members receive project status as soon as it is posted.

Day-to-Day Work

Teams must look at daily operations and determine where potential problems might occur, because the possibility of missed communication is always high. Identifying potential trouble spots can alleviate many of a team's problems. For example, a salesperson who lacks knowledge of what others on the team are doing may be embarrassed to learn that he has just promised something that he can't deliver, because of heavy demands on stock.

Quality of the Relationship

Getting there should be fun and engaging. People should enjoy working together. If they don't, if people aren't laughing or energetic, your team may have serious problems. Some of these relationship factors are:

- *Fun.* Good teams enjoy themselves. Bad teams don't. Fun does not imply that people are always standing around telling jokes, but people should be smiling, teasing each other occasionally, and seeing the lightness in what they do.
- *Listening.* Team members pay attention to the opinions and feelings of their colleagues and respond to them with respect.
- *Encouraging.* People support and bolster each other and take delight in each other's successes.
- *Sharing resources.* People search for ways to work cooperatively. The new supply of photocopy paper is divided among those who need it and not hoarded by the first to find it.
- *Pitching in.* Team members fill in for others and share some of the burden. Members realize that they all work toward a common goal and it is in all of their interests to see that the work gets done.

I'm just a ball player with one ambition, and that is to give all I've got to help my ball club. I've never played any other way.

— Joe DiMaggio

The 10,000-Mile Checkup

Even well-run, joy-to-behold teams need a diagnostic tune-up occasionally. Without frequent checkups the team may fail when you most need it. You may recall the commercial in which a mechanic standing under the lift in his garage tells us about the importance of having a good oil filter, then adds, as he looks at the car on the lift, "You can pay me now or you can pay me later." 10,000-mile checkups save us from the pain of "paying later." Teams that neglect routine maintenance always pay later.

Use the categories of mission and goals, roles and responsibilities, coordination with other teams, approach, day-to-day work, and quality of the relationship to guide your discussion. Simply ask team members to assess your skill at attending to these issues. Celebrate the successful incidents and identify strategies for fixing problem areas.

Frequent tune-ups reduce the chance of major breakdowns. Unfortunately, few teams that are working well want to *waste* time discussing something so soft and touchy-feely as how they are working together. Too bad.

When the Team Breaks Down

Sometimes a tune-up can't anticipate all potential problems, and the team breaks down. Effective teams use this breakdown as an opportunity to learn something about the team and to take corrective actions. Dysfunctional teams pick scapegoats, bitch and moan, throw up their hands, and mumble.

The steps to take:

1. Define the context; identify a particular project or event. Don't discuss the team's work in general — be specific. "Let's discuss the recent problem with our major client, the XYZ Corporation. They complain that the quality of our service has dropped during the past few months."

2. Make certain everyone understands the problem. Clarify until you bleed. Do not try to solve an ill-defined problem. If you don't have enough information to proceed, get the information.

3. Identify all the actions that might be contributing to the problem. Do this without blaming. You are not interested in nailing Harry for this goof (well, maybe you are, but forget about it); you are interested in examining problems dispassionately.

   Try brainstorming. It allows you to list causes quickly and without judgment. Push to get all possible causes listed. If you find that you lack sufficient information to list causes, get the information before proceeding. If you don't have the information, you run the risk of solving an easily identifiable symptom and not the real problem.

4. Determine which of the causes are major contributors.

5. Determine action steps that will correct the problems. Assign responsibilities for making certain the steps are followed. Assign target dates. Determine a way of monitoring progress.

The New Team

Most teams go through predictable stages. Understanding these stages helps you anticipate challenges and keep the team running at full speed. Think of these stages as a three-speed transmission.

First gear. First gear allows the car to start moving from a dead stop. The first-gear needs of a team include attending to all of the criteria listed above: mission and goals, roles and responsibilities, coordination with others, approach, day-to-day work, and quality of the relationships. The team must make certain that its mission is clear, that roles are assigned and understood, and so forth.

Most teams begin in third gear. They jump in the car and hope to hit freeway speed immediately. These teams sputter, and sometimes stall, before getting up to speed. Use of the lower gears does not waste valuable time; it quickens the time it takes to work productively.

Second gear. Second gear allows the car to pick up speed. Teams begin to see what the road is like, see the reality of the challenges, and adjust ways of operating accordingly. For example, the team may find that it must change its way of gathering information or streamline its response to problems.

The team in second gear should pay special attention to all the decisions it made in first gear. Do the roles make sense? Are problems analyzed in the most effective manner?

Third gear. Third gear is used for traveling at top speed. All systems are coordinated and operating smoothly, allowing the team to work with maximum efficiency and effectiveness.

Downshifting. When a team reaches third gear, it does not reach it for life. Conditions change — a team member leaves, the central office sends down a new directive, or a budget is cut. Any change, including confusion among staff over work to be done, is a signal to downshift until the team can pick up speed again. You would never drive up a steep hill in high gear, nor should you try to maintain top speed when the team is facing major struggles. Take the time to slow down and examine how the team is working.

Keeping an Old Clunker on the Road

Some teams are like Chevy Corvairs and will always need lots of work just to keep running. If you own a clunker, then you must take care of it. Pay attention to every rattle and ping and do everything possible to keep the car running smoothly. You may never enjoy the ride or win a road race, but you can at least keep it on the road.

The considerations listed in this chapter are the tools you must use to keep the team running. You may not want to spend time discussing mission and goals with members of this team, but you have little choice. Clunkers need clear direction, tender-loving care, and constant attention.

Relationships among team members are complex. It is often difficult for us to admit our own complicity in a problem; it is tidier to blame others for the faults of the team. As hard as it may be, you should look at yourself as a significant part of that team. Ask, "What am I doing to contribute to this problem?"

Team Building and the Road to Hell

Beware of these scenarios as you work to create a well-functioning team.

The myth of the Dodge Dart. They say Dodge Darts will run forever. These wonderful old cars suffer all manner of abuse and neglect and still keep running. If you've ever worked on one of those invincible Dodge Dart teams, you may think that all teams should run without effort on your part. Most teams are not Darts — they must be maintained.

But we've got work to do. Stopping to examine a team's working process may seem like a luxury when you are swamped with work. But routine maintenance will save you from paying later. Most teams fail because they focus exclusively on what they are doing and never on how they are doing it.

16

Coordinating the Work

In the world of music, conductors are the heroes — the key piece that brings it all together and takes you from mediocrity and just average orchestral maneuvers to greatness. Maybe we've got to look outside of business to define our roles.

— Robb Webb
Vice President,
AVCO Financial Services

In work units where employees take on maximum responsibility for production and quality assurance, the manager finds that his or her role changes significantly. Often a major new responsibility is the coordination of work among individuals and teams. The manager's or supervisor's title may even change to something like "coordinator" or "adviser." In this role, the manager looks at the big picture, working as a liaison among teams, catching duplication of effort, or pushing one group to finish in order to keep its "customer" in the same work unit on schedule.

A coordinator must stay informed. He or she must know when one team is falling behind, another is dangerously low on supplies, or a new and deadlier deadline is about to come down from on high.

If ever there was an argument for management by wandering around, this is it. Managing a group of star performers makes it

151

tempting to steal away to one's own office and delve into pet projects. After all, the team is doing so well, working so efficiently, that
they don't seem to need much supervision. They may not need
direct supervision, but they do need a ringmaster.

Your staff members are your customers. Your job is to make
certain they are able to meet quality and service goals; therefore you
must serve them in whatever way enables them to meet those goals.
As with any customer, you should ask, "How can I serve my customers best?"

Ask them what they need. If you are successful in building a
work unit that is self-directed, they won't let you down. They won't
dump work on you. They will ask for advice, resources, a watchful
eye. They may ask you to be their advocate with another unit or
with the powers on high. They may ask you to mediate a struggle
over who gets the new supply of photocopy paper. You needn't be
clairvoyant — they will tell you what they need if you ask.

The Role of Ringmaster

As ringmaster you may not get high above the big top yourself,
but you can make sure the aerial artists coordinate with the ground
crew so that the net is in place. Look for places where work between
individuals or work groups could break down. For example:

Missed cues. It is easy to do one's work and assume someone
else is taking care of an important detail. Assumptions are killers.
Anticipate where this can occur and build informal structures to
prevent this loss.

Rather than trying to anticipate every contingency and running the risk of creating massive policy treatises, examine the way
you have come. Your unit probably has failed to coordinate well at
least once in its history. Use past experience to inform future
actions. Ask, "What went wrong and how can we guard against its
happening again?"

Duplication of effort. Look for places where well-meaning teams
all set off doing the same task. Your job is to make tough choices —

to tell one team that it cannot propose a particular action. Or, if you like, to mediate the meeting in which they decide who will proceed on a particular project.

Turf battles. Old boundaries erode slowly. You want the entire unit to function as a single team just as the offensive squad, the special teams, and the defensive squad all unite to form a single football team. Turf battles occur when one group feels less powerful than another — when one group feels it is receiving less praise, resources, whatever.

Attitudes. Take a leadership role when problems involving people's feelings and attitudes arise. Retired All-Pro Mark Murphy tells about the fallout at Redskins camp after the 1987 players' strike. Coach Joe Gibbs held a team meeting to clear the air. Little was said. Realizing that silence did not necessarily mean that everything was all right, he called another meeting four hours later. He said that he wanted to get everything out on the table so there would be no bad blood among strikers and those who played during the strike. The meeting did the job. Murphy feels that Gibbs's sensitivity to morale and this meeting in particular were the reasons for the Redskins' ability to put the strike behind them and create team spirit. The Redskins went on to win the Super Bowl that same season.

Staying Informed

Listen for problems. When people complain, use it as an opportunity to learn something. Why are they complaining? Is something breaking down? Does the complaint suggest some action that you should take?

Computer data, spreadsheets, and other reports. You need a way of making sense of information you receive. It helps if you receive data in some consistent format and in a form that everyone, including suppliers and customers, can understand.

The U.S. Agency for International Development requires that all vendors use a particular planning model to present reports. Everyone involved with a U.S. AID project knows how to read the planning document. The costs, intended benefits, time lines, and hazards are described in such a way that even a layperson can grasp the basics of the plan. It makes critique easier, since the reader can compare apples to apples, and it allows everyone involved in the project to see where he or she fits in.

> *We all need continuous help from one another. Interdependence is the greatest challenge.*
>
> — Kurt Lewin

Meetings. Debrief projects. Roll up your sleeves and examine questions of process and productivity — what worked, what didn't? What can be learned from this project? What will be required of each person on subsequent projects? This meeting is not for blaming, it is for learning from experience.

The Road to Hell in Work-Unit Coordination

Watch for a few stumbling blocks as you revise your approach to managing the work in your area.

Doing too good a job. Instead of coordinating, you stick your nose in. You help out. When you find yourself helping, ask if you are doing it as a service (perhaps someone is out sick and the team needs an extra hand) or because you just hate to let go of that pet project. If the latter is true, get out.

Pointing fingers. Instead of learning from the challenges of coordinating work among talented people, you look for scapegoats.

Placing a halo over the group. You believe they are so good that you can leave them alone and do your own work. As we have discussed earlier, that leads to trouble.

Your Relationships with Suppliers and Customers

Expand the boundaries of your team. Often success in meeting quality and service goals can only be achieved by coordinating the efforts of many work units. If you are delegating authority to the maximum extent, then coordination among individuals and units may become one of your major tasks.

One manufacturing company refers to its design and manufacturing process as the "cart by the door" phenomenon. Top management receives an order from a client, places it on a cart, and sends it down to the planning department. Planning determines the schedule and modifications and wheels it down to the manufacturing wing. (I can imagine a group of engineers knocking on the door of manufacturing, giggling, then running back to their offices really fast.) The only time these departments communicate is when something goes wrong — the part is not made to specifications, or a deadline is missed. They spend a significant amount of time fixing things that should have been made correctly to begin with.

You must break down barriers between departments and keep them down. We all tend to be parochial. We look at ourselves and the people who work with us and see only the best. We look at those idiots down in manufacturing and see a group of people who couldn't follow a plan even if it had big pictures. Us versus them kills quality.

A common way to look at an organization's working process is to look at the relationship from the supplier to the work unit to the customer. Everyone has a supplier that provides materials and other resources and a customer who receives the unit's product or service. An accounting office in an investment bank depends on information systems to provide it with fast, reliable software and computers that allow accountants to provide timely and accurate reports to its customer, the corporate senior management team. Complaining about the quality of services coming from information systems or griping about unrealistic deadline expectations from top management accomplishes nothing.

Your role as customer. Many individuals, offices, and companies may see your unit as a customer. Quality and performance problems often occur because of a breakdown in the supplier-to-customer relationship. A late shipment, variable quality, or the wrong size or number of items are but a few of the problems that can occur in this relationship.

Look upon the supplier and your unit as members of a single team; you should work together to meet mutual goals. Companies such as Ford demand that their suppliers meet certain quality standards. They send audit teams into the suppliers' companies to evaluate and make recommendations. This supplier-customer "marriage" is as important between departments within an organization as it is between companies.

The purpose of the audit is not to punish, but to form a partnership that examines problems and attempts to solve them out of mutual self-interest. The customer and supplier share a common goal: The supplier wins by reducing errors and building a strong relationship; the customer gains consistent products or services.

The audit, which may be as simple as a series of candid conversations, should look at the customer's role as well. What is your department doing that inhibits quality? Does it give mixed messages to the supplier regarding deadlines, quantity, or quality? Does it determine what it wants after it receives an order? Ask questions, then shut up and listen.

Your role as supplier. You may have more than a single customer — your boss, a department down the hall, an honest-to-God outside paying customer, or the public. You must find ways to make these customers or stakeholders part of your team — or, as IBM does, become part of their team. IBM is legendary for sending its people into a company and approaching client problems as their own. The message they send is, "We exist to serve you, and we are part of your team." The IBM approach could be used just as successfully by a shipping department that invites itself to help the sales group — one of its customers — solve a problem.

Relationships with Your Stakeholders

Build relationships. You should strive to create a relationship in which your customers can come to your team with problems and suggestions. Building trust takes time. They must learn that you genuinely want to hear their views and that you will do whatever possible to make them happy.

Ask customers when you plan. When Capitol Holding Company of Louisville began moving toward self-directed regional teams, the company called in customers to meet with them for three days. Customers were delighted to give the time, since Capitol's success would give them better service. Customer input gave the company valuable insight into how it should structure these teams to best serve customers.

Increasingly, management information systems departments are regarding other departments within the organization as their customers. This is a major shift from the days when MIS could force systems onto the rest of the organization with impunity. With a customer focus, MIS must work differently. It must speak without jargon and listen to the customer.

Focus groups. Focus groups are widely used in marketing as a means of soliciting input quickly from a variety of potential users. The same approach used by companies such as Stew Leonard's Dairy, which meets regularly with customers to discuss problems and possibilities, can work for offices within a company.

Focus groups may meet once or on a regular basis depending on the purpose. The goal is to find ways to learn from the users of your services so that you can improve your service to them. Although there are no set guidelines for one of these meetings, it does help to prepare questions that focus the discussion on key business issues. Give sufficient time on the agenda for unscheduled conversation; this is where you may learn about significant blind spots.

The focus group meeting should give you a lot to think about. Take it a step further and invite customers to help in problem solving. Remember, you and your customer share a common goal — it is in the interest of both parties to solve problems.

The charette. The simplest way to open communications is to call a meeting in which representatives from each department identify areas that require cooperation. Identify the major breakdowns among units — such as leaving the cart by the door. Determine what the receivers of the cart need; perhaps they need to talk with those delivering the engineering plans to make certain they understand the instructions. Devise a simple strategy to solve this problem.

Keep it specific. Avoid global "we'll-do-better-next-time" pronouncements. Demand specific "on-Monday-morning-we-will-do-X-Y-and-Z" statements.

Architects use meetings called charettes to get input from interested parties as they plan projects. All possible stakeholders are invited to comment on development plans in a single mass meeting. The charette gives the planners an incredible amount of data and a variety of opinions quickly. Some school systems have had good luck in using this technique to open their planning processes to parents, community leaders, students, and school staff.

The charette works best when the presenting group offers a specific idea or plan for consideration, giving interested parties something specific to respond to. For example, the presenting group might send out its plan prior to the meeting. Once the meeting begins, like-minded groups or individuals meet to record their comments on flip charts. Each group presents its comments, allowing time for discussion. A facilitator helps focus the discussion and assists the group in identifying common concerns and areas of agreement.

Although these meetings run the risk of being loud and intense affairs, it is far better to address differences during the planning phase than to wait for unpredictable reactions later.

Keep lines of communication open. I hesitate to suggest regular interdepartmental staff meetings, since they can easily become meaningless. But in the hands of a skilled leader these meetings can be crisply conducted, giving people the information they need and an opportunity to discuss and solve problems.

Create a common language. Problems occur when suppliers, customers, and other stakeholders use different language to describe the same thing. Jargon or arcane planning documents may work fine within a single office but not in communicating across office walls. The Agency for International Development's planning tool, LogFrame, gives contractors, internal offices, and project directors in developing countries a common focal point and language.

The visual model is simple and lends itself to everything from a project to eradicate killer bees in populated areas of Guyana to internal strategic plans. Once someone understands the logic of the model, they can easily understand the basics of a particular approach to a project. Supplier and customer work from a common set of rules, and everyone involved in the project, from project director to the person who will spray the insecticide, understands what will happen and why.

Surveys. When the number of stakeholders is large, written responses can give you a lot of information quickly. That's the good part. Surveys can fail when they are poorly worded and don't elicit information in a form you can use. For instance, simply learning that a customer is unhappy with your product doesn't tell you much. The survey must allow the respondents to tell you precisely where the problems are.

I prefer face-to-face meetings over surveys when possible. Talking with someone allows me to ask follow-up questions and verify my understanding of what they are saying. Written responses often don't tell how much importance to place on a particular item or leave me guessing as to the person's intent.

Involve your staff in these contacts. People on your staff must see how the work they do relates to the work of the other units. Search for ways to include them in the relationship with stakeholders.

Encourage contact. Everyone should be free to talk directly with suppliers, customers, and other stakeholders. Your role should be to make sure interdepartmental meetings, focus groups, surveys, and so forth take place. You don't have to take responsibility for running all of them. Determine who has a need to know and allow those people to meet with their counterparts. It is not uncommon to see hourly workers in an auto assembly plant call their customer in a sister plant miles away, or hear of dental hygienists meeting directly with equipment manufacturers.

Encouraging contact makes sense. Dental hygienists know what they use and where the problems are. They are the best people to talk with suppliers. People on the sales floor need to know what customers want. Filtering information through some Byzantine corporate management chain wastes time and increases the chances that the data gathered will not be the data that the end user needs.

Abolish ceremony. Encourage people from other departments to abolish formal reporting mechanisms and instead come directly to you or your staff when they have a problem. Attempt to do the same in working with their department, taking care not to move too quickly or step on toes. The key is to make it easy for others to talk with you.

When someone from the department down the hall comes to you, delegate the discussion to the person who can best handle it. For political reasons you may choose to sit in on the initial meetings to assure the customer that you are concerned, but do everything possible to wean the customer from you onto your surrogate. Delegating gives the customer a direct line to the person who can solve his or her problem or answer his or her question. This does not preclude you from coordinating work among staff or deciding which customer demand is the higher priority; it simply makes day-to-day work simpler and more convenient. It also gives you time to do other things.

The Road to Hell In Coordinating with Other Units

Again, there are pitfalls to avoid in trying to develop true partnerships with your customers and stakeholders.

Meetings that skitter off into oblivion. Formal interdepartmental meetings may lose their focus. Years ago I was designing a course on team development and used a draft of the materials with an interdepartmental team of a large nonprofit organization. As I asked them to examine topics such as roles and responsibilities, decision-making procedures, and so forth, I received blank stares. Then I asked, "Why do you folks meet every week?" No one could answer the question. Apparently, well before any of the current members had started coming to these weekly meetings, the organization had a good reason for initiating them, but none of the current members had heard of that reason. If you meet, make certain everyone knows why you are meeting and what you hope to accomplish.

Us versus them. The us versus them controversy can be rekindled by the slightest breeze — negative rumors, memos, overheard conversations can do it. You and your colleagues can never take newly earned *glasnost* for granted. You must be diligent in keeping the channels of communication open.

It is easy and a common practice to blame the customer for our shortcomings. I know it's hard to get good customers these days, but you will have to work at it.

Turf battles. When Department A refuses to cooperate or share information with Department B in providing service to a customer, coordination of the whole effort suffers. Citicorp talks about offering "seamless" service to customers. The customers don't care who's not speaking to whom this week or who should get credit. They simply want what they want, without hassle.

Overcoordinating. The temptation for managers is to control everything and have their fingers in every discussion and every decision. Avoid that temptation. It takes too much time and sabotages the independence you wish to engender.

Philip Crosby talks about the "hassle-free" workplace. Think of your job as chief de-hassler for those who work with you.

17

Keeping Yourself Informed

I want people to tell me the truth, even if it costs them their jobs.

— Samuel Goldwyn

In Pirandello's play *Henry IV*, an aristocrat hits his head during a game of polo and awakens believing he is Henry IV, an emperor of the Holy Roman Empire. Not only does no one correct him, but the artifice is maintained by servants who inform guests of the parts they must play to maintain the illusion. Organizations suffer from too many such emperors, as minions run about protecting the boss from the bad news that he or she may be causing their problems.

Too often communication goes from top to bottom with no way for staff to tell the boss that there is a better way. Two major factors contribute to this problem: a natural deference to authority, and fear.

Most people defer to authority. We've been raised to listen to our parents, teachers, and elders. After years of submission, is it any wonder that "subordinates" are reluctant to speak up and tell "superiors" about problems or question instructions? Nowhere is this more true than in the relationship between doctors and nurses. Here is a true story. A man was in a hospital for an ear infection. The doctor, on entering the room, was surprised to find a nurse applying eardrops to the man's buttocks. Both the patient and the nurse knew why the patient was in the hospital, yet they deferred to the doctor's written instructions that explicitly stated, "Apply drops to R ear." [1]

Fear can strike deep. If an employee feels he has just been hit by the wrath of God the one time he dares to confront you, that should effectively keep him from ever coming to you again. A manager in a small company told me that old-timers warn new employees never to disagree with the president. Those who forget this advice find their career advancement opportunities severely diminished.

Few organizations encourage two-way performance feedback. Consequently, few managers ever hear about the things they are doing that get in the way of the work. This top-down approach creates Henry IV kingdoms with no one willing to openly question the king.

Even if you are a fair boss, the superior-subordinate power difference is so significant that you must pay attention to it. People must be encouraged to speak up and be supported when they take that risk.

Remember, before your employees met you, they probably worked for some pretty hellish bosses. You've got to help them, encourage them by demonstrating that you are different, and tell them that you truly want to hear what they have to say.

> *It is the duty of loyal vassals to tell their lords the truth in its proper shape and essence without enlarging on it out of flattery or softening it for any idle reason. I would have you know, Sancho, that if the naked truth were to come to the ears of princes, unclothed in flattery, this would be a different age.*
>
> — Don Quixote

What It Takes

Open door and on the floor. The more accessible you are, the more likely someone is to stop you and make a comment that could give you information on quality or service — or information that could improve your performance. An employee might point out a problem on the line or make a suggestion that indicates you are giving poor instructions.

Ask for advice. Many have written that the organizational pyramid must be turned upside-down, placing those closest to the product or the customer at the top of the chart. This means that everyone else, including managers, should work in service to those people. If you believe this, then you might ask of your staff, "How can I be of more help to you?" Don't expect big things at first — people are likely to be leery of this newfound openness. They will probably suspect that you just read a book on management or went to a workshop, and they may be somewhat suspicious of your new religion.

Self-criticism. The more people see you criticizing your own performance, the more likely they are to offer comments. Turn your mistakes into learning opportunities for the staff.

Team assessments. Assemble the team to discuss the way in which you work — the working process of the team. Discuss what works and what doesn't. This meeting should not cause people to point fingers, but to recognize problems and offer possible solutions.

Reward criticism. When people offer a critique of your work, thank them. You need not agree with their assessment to thank them. Get back to them and tell them how you plan to use the information they gave you — or explain to them why you will not be using their advice. Show respect for the person bringing the news.

Most of us know enough not to kill the messenger, but we will allow him to die of starvation. He offers his message and then hears nothing. The messenger is left thinking: Did I make a mistake telling him? Should I pack my bags?

Informal suggestion box. No, really. You recall Scottsdale, Arizona's "This Seems Dumb to Me" sheet that anyone can complete anonymously. Of course, management must comment on these suggestions and take action when appropriate.

One division head sought anonymous comments and questions regarding a controversial new program he was considering. At a full staff meeting he addressed every question candidly and then gave employees a copy of a list he had compiled of questions and answers. His openness dispelled many of the fears, since people then had real information.

Survey feedback. Many training and development companies offer survey questionnaires that assess management performance on issues such as planning, motivation, and technical knowledge. They can be eye-opening and quite helpful. Consider the following before using one:

Examine the items on the questionnaire. Will it measure the management practices on which you need feedback? If a questionnaire focuses primarily on performance in face-to-face meetings and you work with your staff over modems and phones, you may need to search elsewhere for a questionnaire.

Be wary of questionnaires that use adjectives such as "forceful," "directive," or "supportive." Adjectives are subject to too many varied interpretations. You may end up feeling bad without the benefit of learning what you can do differently. What possible good can it do to learn that 20 percent of your staff feel you are "adaptable" — and that they don't like it? What does "adaptable" mean? What should you change? Look for items that delineate precisely what you are doing right and wrong.

Determine how many people will fill out the questionnaire. The federal government offers managers a well-written feedback tool that gives the manager a comparative score showing self-report together with what the boss has to say. Unfortunately, getting feedback from one person is far too limited. What if that person happens to be a jerk? Look for questionnaires that allow you to give them to multiple bosses, direct reports, and peers.

Get help in interpreting the results. Survey feedback can be overwhelming. Work with someone who can help you understand the responses. Your human resources department may be able to offer this service, and some vendors who sell survey questionnaires offer consultation.

Conversation as a Tool

Perhaps the simplest and ultimately the most effective tool is a conversation with your staff regarding your leadership practices. A focused conversation sends the clear signal that you want feedback from staff. Think of it as a pressure valve on a boiler that releases steam to avert an explosion.

Schedule the meeting so that neither you nor your staff will be interrupted with calls or urgent assignments.

You might use a feedback questionnaire such as the following to gauge how others perceive your leadership practices. If so, ask individuals to complete the questionnaire prior to the meeting and have someone tally the results so that you cannot link an individual to a particular score. The 1 to 7 scale simply makes it easier for people to begin the discussion before giving you specific examples, and the number rating gives you the lay of the land. If everyone rates you "7," you know that things are quite good on that issue and you can move to the next item fairly quickly. (Of course, it could mean that everyone was too petrified to give you anything less.) However, if people's ratings are spread all over the scale, you will need to spend time determining why perceptions are so different and what impact this is having on productivity and morale.

> *My first message is listen, listen, listen to the people who do the work.*
>
> — H. Ross Perot

Leadership Practices Questionnaire

1. Setting Direction

A. How well do I state and clarify vision, goals, and objectives?

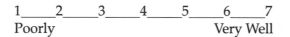

1____2____3____4____5____6____7
Poorly   Very Well

Examples:

What could I do to improve?

B. How well do I lead by example? Do my actions demonstrate a commitment to employee involvement?

1____2____3____4____5____6____7
Poorly   Very Well

Examples:

What could I do to improve?

2. Keeping Others Informed

A. Do I give you helpful and timely feedback regarding your performance?

1____2____3____4____5____6____7
Rarely   Often

Examples:

What could I do to improve?

B. How well do I keep you informed of changes in the business or the work of other units?

1____2____3____4____5____6____7
Poorly   Very Well

Examples:

What could I do to improve?

3. Initiative

A. How well do I encourage you to take risks?

1____2____3____4____5____6____7
Poorly   Very Well

Examples:

What could I do to improve?

B. How well do I use failed risks as learning opportunities (do I punish the risk taker)?

1_____2_____3_____4_____5_____6_____7
Poorly   Very Well

Examples:

What could I do to improve?

4. Support

A. Do I give you sufficient support and encouragement?

1_____2_____3_____4_____5_____6_____7
Rarely   Often

Examples:

What could I do to improve?

B. Does this support feel sincere?

1_____2_____3_____4_____5_____6_____7
Rarely   Often

Examples:

What could I do to improve?

5. Development

A. How well do I provide the help you need to develop skills to do your job?

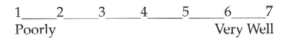

1_____2_____3_____4_____5_____6_____7
Poorly   Very Well

Examples:

What could I do to improve?

B. How well do I provide support for your career development?

1_____2_____3_____4_____5_____6_____7
Poorly   Very Well

Examples:

What could I do to improve?

6. Coordinating Effort

A. How effectively am I coordinating work within this work unit?

1_____2_____3_____4_____5_____6_____7
Poorly   Very Well

Examples:

What could I do to improve?

B. How efficiently am I coordinating work between you and our suppliers and customers?

1_____2_____3_____4_____5_____6_____7
Poorly   Very Well

Examples:

What could I do to improve?

7. Building a Team

How well do I encourage the development of your work team?

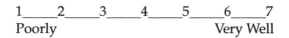

1_____2_____3_____4_____5_____6_____7
Poorly   Very Well

Examples:

What could I do to improve?

8. Keeping Yourself Informed

How easy is it for you to criticize me?

1_____2_____3_____4_____5_____6_____7
Impossible   Easy

Examples:

What could I do to improve?

In each category you should be looking for a critique — both positive and negative — and ideas. If people say you fail to coordinate the effort among staff, ask what they would prefer. Tell staff how you will use the feedback you have received. You might say that they have given you a lot to think about and you will get back to them in a week with your plan for coordinating effort more effectively.

The first time you use this tool, expect that people will be reluctant to talk. They'll wonder, "What's she up to?" Be prepared to prime the pump. For instance, if you think you have been somewhat weak on giving direction and feedback, you might say, "I've been on the road a lot during the past few months, and I don't feel I've done a very good job of giving you direction or critique. Is that a fair assessment?" Candor on your part makes it much safer for people to respond.

Whatever the results of the first conversation, thank your staff. Then do it again sometime. The more you do it, the easier it becomes for you and your staff.

Critique and the Road to Hell

Watch for traps that can keep you from getting the feedback you need.

You know you don't need it. Since everyone knows that IQs jump 25 points with each promotion, what possible need could you have for information regarding the work or your performance? Even though you don't need it, what the hell, what have you got to lose?

Overreacting. Instead of thanking the messenger, the manager reacts by punishing her. Often this may come out as a defensive response to the criticism, such as mounting a counterattack against the employee ("You know, you're no jewel yourself!") or inundating her with the hundreds of reasons why she is wrong.

The black hole. People offer you some criticism. You listen stoically, without responding. Never is another word spoken about it. Don't keep your employees in the dark, wondering, "What did the boss think? Am I persona non grata for telling him?" Thank your staff. You need not agree with the comments to thank the messengers.

Too much too soon. If your staff has never given you any critique or commented in any way on how things are done, don't expect high-quality comments at first. People will play their cards close to their vests, and rightly so. They can't afford to show too much of their hand until you play yours.

Showing you are willing to hear that you are not the omnipotent Henry IV is perhaps the single most important leadership skill you can use. Your willingness to accept and take criticism to heart shows that you really are concerned about true partnership, and it creates a climate in which others feel that they can begin asking for candid critique.

Afterword

Managing a ball club is the most vulnerable job in the world . . . If you don't win you're going to be fired. If you do win, you only put off the day when you're going to be fired. And no matter what you do, you're going to be second-guessed. The manager is the only person in the ball park who has to call it right now. Everybody else can call it after it's over.

— Leo Durocher
Nice Guys Finish Last[1]

Is that all there is to it — simply read this book and the heavens will open, admitting you to the pantheon of the all-time great managers? You know the answer. You will never arrive. You may find some wonderful spots along the way, but the journey never ends. Conditions change. Just when you are about to settle into an easy relationship with your staff, corporate headquarters lays off scores of employees. Just when quality and customer satisfaction seem to be as good as humans could hope for, a new competitor enters the market and seriously damages your earnings. And on and on it goes.

Chapter 3 discussed NUMMI's seemingly miraculous renewal. As impressive as NUMMI's high productivity, high quality, and high worker commitment are, it could come crumbling down around them. Some workers complain that work schedules are brutal, that involvement may be a way of extracting more for less. If NUMMI managers are wise, they will pay attention to these signals, renew the partnership between management and employees, and take corrective action. As I finished this book, Nordstrom was reportedly suffering from labor management problems in Washington State. We can only hope that Nordstrom will be, as John Gardner puts it, a "renewing organization," one that faces changing conditions and problems openly while maintaining its traditional values.

The sad paradox is that trust is difficult to build and easy to destroy. The same forces that led to divisiveness between labor and management or to the mind-numbing alienation of the large bureaucracy could easily and quickly rise again. To contend with these forces, we cannot deny their existence; we must constantly search for their signs and take action to keep partnership alive. Everyone has a responsibility to keep the lines of communication open, dispel rumors, and engage in conflict directly and candidly. We are human and fallible; we make mistakes. Assume that this is true and take these setbacks in stride.

I began this book stating that we have the potential to create work environments that can transform the nature of work. The burden of success or failure rests in large part on the shoulders of supervisors and middle-level managers. You who are members of these ranks must create ways to implement processes that champion the commitment to quality and service while increasing the possibility for people to find dignity and meaning in their work. That is quite a challenge, but the benefits to organizations and individuals are enormous.

You are not alone. Many in private industry, nonprofits, and government are fighting the good fight — sometimes winning, sometimes losing, but always giving us ideas to inform our actions. Those who are doing it right are willing to help us. They open their doors to visitors. They answer questions with amazing candor. They want others to succeed. They understand that it's not just about profits or quality control charts; it's about bringing dignity and respect to the workplace.

Any real change implies the breakup of the world as one has always known it, the loss of all that gave one identity, the end of safety, and at such a moment, unable to see and not daring to imagine what the future will bring forth, one clings to what one knew, or thought one knew; to what one possessed or dreamed that one possessed. Yet it is only when a man is able, without bitterness or self-pity to surrender a dream he has long cherished, or a privilege he has long possessed, that he is set free — that he has set himself free — for higher dreams, for greater privileges.

— James Baldwin
Nobody Knows My Name

Notes

Opening quote

Thomas Jefferson, letter to William Charles Jarvis, September 28, 1820.

1 Managing in a World without Rules

1. Jamie Houghton quote from *Quality Progress*, March 1987.
2. Robert Levering, *A Great Place to Work* (New York: Random House, 1989), 260.
3. Philip Crosby, *Quality without Tears: The Art of Hassle-free Management* (New York: McGraw-Hill, 1984), 5.
4. Joel Barker, *Discovering the Future: The Business of Paradigms* (St. Paul: Ili Press, 1985).

Note: Many books and articles cover this new terrain. You might try Michael L. Dertouzos, et al., *Made in America: Regaining the Productive Edge* (Cambridge, Mass.: MIT Press, 1989) or Peter Drucker, *The New Realities* (New York: Harper and Row, 1989).

2 Traveling the Road to Hell

1. W. Edwards Deming, *Out of the Crisis* (Cambridge, Mass.: MIT Press, 1988), 102.
2. Philip Crosby, *Quality without Tears: The Art of Hassle-free Management* (New York: McGraw-Hill, 1984), 19.

Note: All Road to Hell examples attributed to specific organizations come from public sources such as newspapers and the business press. For obvious reasons, I have not disclosed the identity of companies in other Road to Hell examples in which the story was either told to me or was a hellish act I witnessed firsthand.

3 Our Desire to Be Involved

1. Quoted during a National Public Radio interview.
2. Terry made this comment during a jazz workshop I attended at Howard University in 1973.
3. Douglas McGregor, *The Human Side of Enterprise* (New York: McGraw-Hill, 1960).
4. Gordon Forward, quoted in "Wide open management at Chaparral Steel," *Harvard Business Review,* May/June 1986, 99.
5. Tom Peters, *Thriving on Chaos* (New York: Knopf, 1987), 282.

Note: The purpose of this chapter is merely to remind you of the principle themes of motivation. For a further exploration of the topic, you might consider Victor Frankl, *Man's Search for Meaning* (Pocket Books, 1959) or J. A. Shotgren, ed., *Models for Management* (The Woodlands, Tex.: Teleometrics, 1980). The second book includes classic articles on the subject of motivation by McGregor, Herzberg, Argyris, Maslow, and Livingston.

4 Considering the Options

1. Japan Human Relations Association, ed., *The Idea Book: Improvement through TEI (Total Employee Involvement)* (Cambridge, Mass.: Productivity Press, 1988), 201.

2. *Ibid.*, pp. xiii to xv.
3. Bill Dickinson, ed., *TEI Newsletter* (Cambridge, Mass: Productivity, Inc.)
4. Max DePree, *Leadership Is an Art* (New York: Doubleday, 1989).

Note: The proliferation of examples and unique approaches quickly outdates any list of options. We should be thankful for that — every day there are more and more organizations we can learn from. However, the Resources section in the Appendix does list newsletters, videos, and books that give examples of good practices. Also, I highly recommend conferences such as those presented by the Association for Quality and Participation or Productivity, Inc., for meeting other people who are struggling with the issues of involvement.

5 Assessing Yourself

Note: There is no shortage of management assessment instruments on the market. My favorite is the *Management Skills Profile*, published by Personnel Decisions, Inc., Minneapolis, MN. The questionnaire is thorough, practical, and easy to interpret. But these assessment tools should not become substitutes for face-to-face, candid conversations about performance issues. You might prime the pump with an assessment and then begin building practices that will provide you with "emperor's new clothes" feedback on a regular basis.

6 Creating a Partnership

1. Paul Dickson quoted in William Safire and Leonard Safir, *Words of Wisdom: More Good Advice* (New York: Simon & Schuster, 1989), 131.
2. Peter Block, *The Empowered Manager* (San Francisco: Jossey-Bass, 1987), discussion on pp. 130-151. Block has written a wonderful book that gets to the heart of the difficulties we face in creating partnerships with others. I encourage you to read it.
3. From "Labor Letter," *Wall Street Journal*, January 24, 1989.

7 Beginning the Discussion

1. Joan Didion, quoted in William Safire and Leonard Safir, *Words of Wisdom: More Good Advice* (New York: Simon & Schuster, 1989), 200.
2. From the *Washington Monthly*, June 1986, as quoted by Tom Peters in *Thriving on Chaos* (New York: Knopf, 1987), 285.

8 Identifying the Values

1. *Wall Street Journal*, January 30, 1989.

9 Pulling It All Together

1. From a talk delivered at the 1991 conference of the Association for Quality and Participation.
2. Force-field analysis was created by Kurt Lewin (1890-1947) to show how forces acting against each other limit our ability to change. Lewin's research on motivation predates much of American business's newfound knowledge about employee involvement by some fifty years. For more on Lewin's work, try Alfred Marrow, *The Practical Theorist* (New York: Basic Books, 1969).

10 Providing Direction

1. I interviewed Edwin Locke for an American Red Cross videotape production in 1982. To learn more about their work, you might read their article, "Goal Setting: A Motivation Technique that Works," in *Organizational Dynamics*, Autumn 1979, 68-80.
2. Robert Waterman, Jr., *The Renewal Factor* (New York: Bantam, 1988).
3. Described by a BBC producer at an International Television and Video Association conference.
4. Ricardo Semler, "Managing without Managers," *Harvard Business Review*, September/October, 1989, 79.

11 Keeping People Informed

1. Tom Peters and Robert Waterman, Jr., *In Search of Excellence* (New York: Harper & Row, 1982), 102.
2. *Wall Street Journal*, January 28, 1988.
3. Philip Crosby, *Quality without Tears: The Art of Hassle-free Management* (New York: McGraw-Hill, 1984), 67.
4. Charles Osborne, *Verdi: A Life in the Theater* (New York: Knopf, 1988), 226.

13 Encouraging Initiative

1. Warren Bennis and Burt Nanus, *Leaders* (New York: Harper & Row, 1985), 76.

14 Helping Employees Develop

1. Miles Davis, *Miles* (New York: Simon & Schuster, 1989), 220.
2. Heinz Pagels, *Dreams of Reason* (New York: Simon & Schuster, 1988), 139.

Note: The situational leadership theory developed by Paul Hersey and Kenneth Blanchard remains a respected standard for describing the relationship between the manager and staff vis-à-vis development. Although the theory lacks any significant research base, it does offer a practical and intuitively appealing way to describe this process. Contact Blanchard Training and Development, Escondido, CA, or University Associates, San Diego, CA, for more information.

15 Building an Effective Team

1. Gordon E. Forward, quoted in "Wide-open management at Chaparral Steel," *Harvard Business Review*, May/June 1986, 100.

Note: For more on this subject, try William Dyer, *Team Building: Issues and Alternatives* (Reading, Mass.: Addison-Wesley, 1987). Also see Peter Scholtes, *The Team Handbook,* which is described in Appendix A. Jack Gibb's article, "Climate for Trust Formation," from *T-Group Theory and Laboratory Method* (New York: John Wiley, 1964), remains the most helpful theory (to me) on how groups develop. The article is long and not focused on business groups, so it lacks an immediate practical application. For starters, try "The Gibb Theory of Group Development," by Sue Brocklebank and myself, in *The Group Development Handbook* (Washington, DC: Mid-Atlantic Association for Training and Consulting, 1990), 7.

17 Keeping Yourself Informed

1. Robert Cialdini, *Influence: The New Psychology of Modern Persuasion* (New York: Quill, 1984), 212-13.

   Note: See the Chapter 5 notes for a description of another assessment questionnaire.

Afterword

1. Leo Durocher quoted in *The Harper Book of American Quotations* (New York: Harper & Row, 1988; Caruth & Erlich, eds.), sec. 30, quote 10.

Closing quote

James Baldwin, "Faulkner and Desegregation," in *Nobody Knows My Name* (New York: Dial Press, 1961), 117.

Appendix A

Resources

> *The purpose of education is to make the young as unlike their parents as possible.*
>
> — Woodrow Wilson
> Former president of the United States
> and Princeton University

The purpose of this book is to help managers act as unlike their predecessors as possible. Here are some books, videos, and audiotapes that can help you make that transition.

Customer Service

Karl Albrecht, *At America's Service* (Homewood, Ill.: Dow Jones-Irwin, 1988). A practical book, filled with suggestions about ways to promote customer service. Albrecht believes in the statement, "Treat your people right and they will treat your customers right."

Robert L. Desatnick, *Managing to Keep the Customer* (San Francisco: Jossey-Bass, 1987). Practical advice on customer service with many real-world examples.

Ron Zemke with Dick Schaaf, *The Service Edge: 101 Companies that Profit from Customer Care* (New York: New American Library,

1989). Profiles of successful companies that promote exemplary customer service. The opening section focuses on themes that distinguish the best from all the others.

Tom Peters, *Thriving on Chaos* (New York: Knopf, 1987). Peters provides lots of illustrations drawn from a variety of businesses and includes many prescriptions for successful practice. The book is comprehensive and could easily have been placed in the section on quality or leadership.

Employee Involvement

Edward E. Lawler III, *High-Involvement Management* (San Francisco: Jossey-Bass, 1986). Lawler gives a thorough assessment of various participative management approaches and examines their history, strengths, weaknesses, and possible applications. The book discusses quality circles, employee survey feedback, job enrichment, work teams, union-management quality of work-life programs, gainsharing, new-design plants, and Lawler's suggestions for managing change in the transition to a high-involvement organization. If you want to explore your options, this is the book for you.

Robert Levering, *A Great Place to Work* (New York: Random House, 1989). Lists the reasons why some places are just what the title says. The points won't surprise you, but they are good reminders. Research cited strongly suggests that these companies do far better in the marketplace than their less-than-great counterparts.

Peter Scholtes, *The Team Handbook* (Madison, Wis.: Joiner Associates, 1988). A guide for teams working on quality improvement issues. This practical and thoughtful book was written for the people who do the work.

Marvin R. Weisbord, *Productive Workplaces: Organizing and Managing for Dignity, Meaning, and Community* (San Francisco: Jossey-Bass, 1987). This is a fine book. In the extensive first part, Weisbord examines four theorists who have influenced our thinking on people's relationship to the workplace. Using historical thinking as a foundation, he moves on in very practical fashion to suggest ways in which we might begin transforming organizations to increase dignity as well as productivity.

Japan Human Relations Association, *The Idea Book: Improvement through TEI (Total Employee Involvement)* (Cambridge, Mass.: Productivity Press, 1988). This book shows you how to use the participative suggestion systems that are integrated with management systems in many Japanese companies; it is practical and outlines specific factors to consider.

Also recommended: *The Service Industry Idea Book: Employee Involvement in Retail and Office Improvement* (Cambridge, Mass.: Productivity Press, 1990) contains similar practical information focused on the service industry.

Karen Jones, ed., *Best of TEI* (Cambridge, Mass.: Productivity Press, 1988). This notebook style book includes the best papers and edited transcripts of presentations made at Productivity's first three TEI Conferences. It provides a broad introduction to many different approaches to involvement, with top management viewpoints, case studies, and materials on training, suggestion systems, and teamwork from such organizations as AT&T Network Systems, Digital Equipment Corporation, Motorola, IBM, and GE Mobile Communications.

Examples of Well-run Organizations

The Tom Peters tapes — he has made a number of fine videos. I particularly like *The Leadership Alliance,* which focuses on the management strategies of leaders in four organizations, and *Excellence in the Public Sector,* which covers improvement efforts in four government organizations and one nonprofit agency. They are available from many video distributors.

Robert H. Waterman, Jr., *The Renewal Factor* (New York: Bantam, 1988). This well-written book by the quieter member of the famous *In Search of Excellence* team is filled with examples of organizations that stay competitive. It also contains ideas for renewing organizations. An added bonus: Waterman is an engaging writer and fun to read.

Bureau of Labor-Management Relations and Cooperative Programs, *The Labor-Management Brief*, U.S. Department of Labor, Washington, D.C. A series of case studies on successful cooperative agreements between management and labor. Well-written, packed with valuable information, and free. The series includes Harley-Davidson, Preston Trucking, NUMMI, and many others.

Ricardo Semler, "Managing without Managers," *Harvard Business Review,* September/October, 1989 (Reprint 89503). Want to spur your thinking? Against formidable odds, Semler revitalized a manufacturing operation in Brazil, where employees now set their own salaries, full democracy in the workplace is a reality, and the company is wildly successful. A nice stocking-stuffer for those "it'll-never-work-here" folks.

Leadership

Peter Block, *The Empowered Manager* (San Francisco: Jossey-Bass, 1987). Perhaps the best book ever written for midlevel managers. Block explores the nature of relationships between managers and subordinates and suggests ways of improving them. The sections on creating a vision and gaining support for ideas are particularly helpful.

Bernard M. Bass, "Leadership: Good, Better, Best," *Organizational Dynamics*, Winter 1985. Bass argues that we need transformational leaders in organizations, rather than managers who can merely carry out daily leadership "transactions." His ideas are worth serious attention.

Warren Bennis and Burt Nanus, *Leaders* (New York: Harper & Row, 1985). A fine anecdotal study of effective leaders. Examples range from Karl Wallenda, the patriarch of the Flying Wallendas, to Thomas Watson, Sr., the founder of IBM.

Max DePree, *Leadership Is an Art* (New York: Doubleday, 1989). DePree is chairman of the Herman Miller Company, one of the companies listed in *100 Great Places to Work.* In this wonderfully inspiring book, he writes about leadership as if the relationship between leader and employee were a sacred covenant — which, of course, it is.

James Kouzes and Barry Posner, *The Leadership Challenge* (San Francisco: Jossey-Bass, 1987). A fine book that examines the attitudes and practices of effective leaders. The emphasis, as you might guess, is on ways of empowering those who follow these leaders. The section on the need for clear vision is particularly effective in describing visions and how they might be created.

John P. Kotter, *The Leadership Factor* (New York: The Free Press, 1988). An examination of what it takes to be an effective manager in a complex organization. Kotter's work is particularly helpful because it demands that we look to the future and examine leadership needs in a changing work environment.

John P. Kotter, *A Force for Change* (New York: The Free Press, 1990). A follow-up to his previous book. Sound advice on why managers must be leaders, too.

Keeping Informed

TEI Newsletter, Productivity, Inc., PO Box 3007, Cambridge, Mass., 02140 (Bill Dickinson, Ed.). TEI stands for Total Employee Involvement. This is a monthly newsletter that combines case studies with opinions on the topic of employee involvement. A recent issue included a profile of employee involvement at Mazda, an interview with Tom Peters, and tips on using incentives wisely. Productivity also sponsors the TEI Institute (a networking organization for managers) and twice-annual TEI Conferences where participants can learn about which methods for increasing employee involvement work and which don't through presentations from leading companies and experts in the field.

Work in America (Washington, D.C.: Buraff Publications). This newsletter covers management and labor relations, employee involvement, and many other related issues.

The Association for Quality and Participation (801-B West 8th Street, Cincinnati, OH 45203). This is the organization to join if you are interested in employee involvement. Semiannual conferences feature workshops by consultants, nationally known keynote speakers, and presentations by management/employee work teams. The work team presentations are the highlights of the conferences.

Quality Improvement

Philip Crosby, *Quality without Tears: The Art of Hassle-Free Management* (New York: McGraw-Hill, 1984). This is a good book that outlines the steps managers must take to "de-hassle" the work environment. Like Deming and Juran, Crosby takes no prisoners in his effort to rid the world of shoddy quality and service.

W. Edwards Deming, *Out of the Crisis* (Cambridge, Mass.: MIT Press, 1988). Deming is the guru of quality. After World War II, Japan listened to him — we didn't. He is crusty, highly opinionated, and — in my mind — right. The book covers his management philosophy.

The Deming Library, Chicago: Films, Inc. (800) 323-4222. This series of 16 videos covers Deming's philosophy. Most helpful are the tapes that focus on quality improvement at Ford and Vernay Laboratories. In the four tapes known as the *Deming User's Manual*, two Deming disciples, Peter Scholtes and Brian Joiner, rail against performance appraisal systems and management by objectives. I found the tapes on performance appraisal particularly good.

Joseph M. Juran, *Juran on Planning for Quality* (New York: The Free Press, 1988). Japan listened to Juran and Deming in the 1950s when the United States was fat and happy. The book breaks down each step in the product development process into a supplier, transformer, and customer sequence. The thoroughness of this analysis helps focus attention on the need for very specific information from suppliers and customers at every step. The book reads more like detailed lecture notes than something intended for print. Nevertheless, Juran's point of view is sound and worth serious consideration.

Other Resources

James Collins and Jerry Porras, "Making Impossible Dreams Come True," *Stanford Business School Magazine*, Summer 1989. A clearly written article that sorts out the differences between vision, mission, and purpose.

Joel Barker, *Discovering the Future: The Business of Paradigms* (St. Paul: Ili Press, 1985). Barker argues that old paradigms — or ways of looking at the world — make it difficult, if not impossible, for us to see the need for change even when it is upon us. A good, readable book with arguments that should compel you to examine just about everything in light of his paradigm premise. Even better is a set of tapes from his speech at the 1988 convention of the Association for Quality and Participation, which begin by covering the same ground as his book. In an informal discussion that follows the speech, Barker goes beyond the ideas presented in the book and suggests ways of getting innovation accepted. Available from ACTS, 14153 Clayton Road, Ballwin, MO 63011.

Appendix B

Assessment Forms

Here are the main diagnostic tools introduced in the text so that you can reproduce blank copies for personal use within your work unit. Please include the book title, publisher, publication date, and author's name on all reproductions.

Although these forms can't cover the details of every situation, they may help identify points of common concern or indicate areas where skills are weak.

Self-Assessment: Am I Ready?

Score your reaction to the following statements, from 1 = you've got to be kidding, to 7 = I couldn't agree more.

Commitment

I believe that pushing maximum control down to the people closest to the product or customer is a wise move. I believe that this will increase the commitment to quality and service among staff and will therefore increase the quality of the work we do.

1_____2_____3_____4_____5_____6_____7

Work Process Skills

I have the skills needed to analyze work flow and statistical quality control, and know how to use problem analysis and problem-solving techniques, such as constructing Pareto charts.

1_____2_____3_____4_____5_____6_____7

Knowledge of Organization

I have a thorough understanding of the reasons why employee involvement is important to our organization and how my unit fits into the move toward higher quality and service.

1_____2_____3_____4_____5_____6_____7

Employee Involvement Orientation

I understand how the various involvement options can be applied and have a good understanding of what can work and what will fail in my type of organization.

1_____2_____3_____4_____5_____6_____7

Leadership Skills

These are the leadership skills you need to build a partnership with your staff. Each skill is discussed at length in the chapters of Part Three.

1. Setting Direction
   A. How well do I state and clarify vision, goals, and objectives?

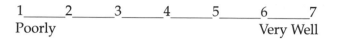

   B. How well do I lead by example? Do my actions demonstrate a commitment to employee involvement?

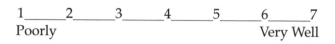

2. Keeping Others Informed
   A. How well do I give helpful and timely feedback regarding performance?

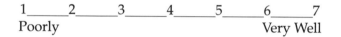

   B. How well do I keep others informed regarding changes in the business or the work of other units?

3. Initiative
   A. How well do I encourage people to take risks?

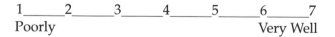

   B. How well do I use failed risks as learning opportunities (or do I punish the risk-taker)?

4. Support
   How well do I give people support and encouragement?

   1_____2_____3_____4_____5_____6_____7
   Poorly   Very Well

5. Development
   A. How well do I provide the help people need to develop skills to do their jobs?

   1_____2_____3_____4_____5_____6_____7
   Poorly   Very Well

   B. How well do I provide support for people's career development?

   1_____2_____3_____4_____5_____6_____7
   Poorly   Very Well

6. Coordinating Effort
   A. How well do I coordinate work within this work unit?

   1_____2_____3_____4_____5_____6_____7
   Poorly   Very Well

   B. How well do I coordinate work between this unit and our suppliers and customers?

   1_____2_____3_____4_____5_____6_____7
   Poorly   Very Well

7. Building a Team
   How well do I encourage the development of a healthy work team?

   1_____2_____3_____4_____5_____6_____7
   Poorly   Very Well

8. Keeping Yourself Informed
   How well do I encourage and accept criticism from others?

   1_____2_____3_____4_____5_____6_____7
   Poorly   Very Well

Interpretation

Commitment

1 to 3 points. Introducing involvement processes may be very difficult for you. Determine whether your low score reflects a distrust in the people currently assigned to you or a basic distrust of this process.

If you are concerned that your staff is not up to this challenge, remember that in many places, managers who swore they were working with turned-off Theory X people before introducing these processes now enjoy an increased partnership and commitment to quality and service.

Identify what it will take for you to increase your commitment to this process. Talk with others who have made it work. Ask them how they got over the initial fear and resistance to change. Take heart: others have been skeptical, too.

Finally, a warning: look to the future. Increasing the partnership between management and staff is gaining in popularity. If that's true in your organization, consider the implications for managers who don't embrace this concept.

4 to 5 points. You may be taking a "wait-and-see" attitude. But if you wait, what you'll see is that nothing will change. Success demands your leadership. Your staff can't lead you.

Learn more about the process and how it has worked. Visit places where it has worked and ask managers tough questions: Do they like the new arrangement? What challenges do they face? Would they go back to the old way if they could?

Determine what it will take for you to increase your commitment to this process.

6 to 7 points. You probably are wondering why the organization waited so long to begin this process. For years you've known it would work.

Work Process Skills

Note: The tools such as statistical process control may not be appropriate to your business. If not, a low score is nothing to worry about. However, problem analysis and decision-making tools can work quite effectively in most settings.

1 to 3 points. If you need these skills in your organization, consider begging the human resources or quality assurance department to offer this training.

4 to 5 points. A refresher course might be in order.

6 to 7 points. Seems as if you are in good shape.

Knowledge of Organization

1 to 5 points. Determine where you must go to get answers to your questions. Some questions you might consider asking:

- Does corporate headquarters have a plan for increasing involvement?
- Does the organization have a set of values or a vision that is guiding its action?
- Who is driving this process? (The CEO? No one?)
- What support and resources can I expect from the organization?
- Have other units within the organization started involvement processes? Have they been successful?

6 to 7 points. You are probably ready to get started.

Employee Involvement Orientation

1 to 5 points. You need more information. Fortunately, many options are available to you. Consider the following:

- Appendix A lists many resources — books, tapes, case studies — that describe employee involvement as well as quality and service improvement issues.
- Other units within your organization may have already struggled with these same issues. Call or visit them and pump them for information — what works, what doesn't, what they would do differently if they could.
- Occasionally, the human resources department will have good information on ways of implementing employee involvement processes.

6 to 7 points. Good luck. Just remember, what worked on Broadway may bomb in Peoria. An involvement process that worked at a General Electric plant cannot be dropped into J.C. Penney and be expected to work. Keep your mind and your options open.

Leadership Skills

Consider each score individually. Don't average the scores. For instance, if you gave yourself a 6 on seven categories and a 1 on a single category, don't assume that you earned a grade of 5.4. Consider the low score separately — it has something to tell you.

1 to 5 points. Effective use of these skills can have a significantly positive impact on the implementation of the involvement process. Examine each category. Take low to mid-range scores seriously. Skip ahead to Part III and read the chapters that discuss your lower scores, and then develop a plan to improve these skills.

6 to 7 points. Feeling smug? Consider giving the questionnaire in Chapter 17 to your staff to see if they agree with your high score.

Starting Points

The conversation topics listed below should help you focus the discussion on issues that can either help or hinder the employee involvement process. Each category lists a positive and a negative statement. Consider these as ends of a continuum. Your organization and work unit will fall somewhere on that scale. For example, if managers at Eastern Airlines had examined the category "management/staff history" in the late 1980s, they would most likely have placed a mark near the low end of the scale, then explained the reason for the score.

1___2 X 3___ 4___ 5___ 6___ 7___ 8___ 9___ 10
Negative   Positive

Explanation of Score:

> *Two major strikes in the past few years. During early days of the machinists' strike, two other unions walked out in sympathy. Former chairman Frank Borman's well-publicized disdain of employee involvement: "I'm not going to have the monkeys running the zoo."*

Management/Staff History

Positive. The organization and this unit have enjoyed a long history of good management/staff (labor) relations.

Negative. Management/staff relations have been tense for a long time. Trust is low on both sides. Suspicion is high whenever management tries something new.

1___ 2 ___3___ 4___ 5___ 6___ 7___ 8___ 9 ___10
Negative   Positive

Explanation of Score:

Organizational Structure

Positive. Senior management encourages a flexible organizational structure. They may direct individual work units to create formal or informal systems that serve the task. Work units are organized in ways that increase quality and efficiency. People are encouraged to cross organizational boundaries or jump levels in the organization to get the job done.

Negative. The organization is highly bureaucratic. Titles and the chain of command are strictly adhered to. Turf wars may reign between departments.

1___2___3___4___5___6___7___8___9___10
Negative   Positive

Explanation of Score:

Values and Vision

Positive. Senior management offers a clear and consistent message of values and vision, and these statements are consistent with the principles of employee involvement. Senior management champions these values and promotes their use to inform the actions throughout the organization.

Negative. If senior management provides any statement of vision, it is generally believed to be only lip service. Organizational practices, despite words to the contrary, largely reflect Theory X.

1___2___3___4___5___6___7___8___9___10
Negative   Positive

Explanation of Score:

Communication

Positive. The organization encourages open communication. In keeping with the maxim that truth can come from anywhere, no restriction is put on a person's freedom to criticize or suggest. All employees are given information about the organization's performance in open forums — such as quarterly meetings with question and answer sessions and discussions about the anticipated direction the organization may take. An honest attempt is made to address rumors. People receive timely and helpful feedback.

Negative. Information is closely held. Often even those with a practical need to know don't get the information required to make informed decisions. People are frequently in the dark with regard to their own performance.

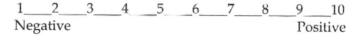

1____2____3____4____5____6____7____8____9____10
Negative   Positive

Explanation of Score:

Customer Focus

Positive. The organization bases its evaluation of performance on the customers' reactions to products and services. This customer orientation extends to external as well as internal customers.

Negative. Evaluations are internal. Each unit evaluates its own performance based on internal criteria, such as the information services department that rates its work based on its own perceptions rather than on evaluations by the recipients of the service. The organization may blame customers for its own failures.

```
1____2____3____4____5____6____7____8____9____10
Negative                                    Positive
```

Explanation of Score:

Skills

Positive. The people of this work unit have the skills needed to serve customers well. The staff are capable of identifying problems, working on practical solutions, anticipating needs, and completing the highest quality of work without close supervision.

Negative. For any number of reasons, people lack the training to do the job right or take on greater responsibility.

```
1____2____3____4____5____6____7____8____9____10
Negative                                    Positive
```

Explanation of Score:

Commitment

Positive. Senior management has shown real commitment to the process of employee involvement. They provide direction, resources, and support for managers and work units that attempt to apply more participatory approaches.

Negative. Employee involvement is believed to be just a passing fad, a "flavor of the month." Few take the talk of participation seriously.

1___2___3___4___5___6___7___8___9___10
Negative   Positive

Explanation of Score:

Driving Force

Positive. Some external driving force is pushing the organization to examine its practices regarding quality and service. For instance, the company may be facing severe competition from Japanese manufacturing or anticipating a new threat to markets from the European community.

Negative. There is nothing pushing improvement at this time. A large government bureaucracy may believe it is immune from public calls for higher quality, or a company may believe that it has no serious competition and therefore no reason to change.

1___2___3___4___5___6___7___8___9___10
Negative   Positive

Explanation of Score:

Manager's Role

Positive. Managers and supervisors are expected to provide participatory leadership. They are given training and encouragement to involve people to a greater degree.

Negative. Managers are rewarded solely on bottom-line performance. They may be encouraged to monitor the work of staff very closely, and are held accountable if a staff member takes a risk and fails.

1____2____3____4____5____6____7____8____9____10
Negative   Positive

Explanation of Score:

Quality and Service Standards

Positive. The organization has clear and specific ways by which to measure quality and service. Quality, not quantity, is valued. When a problem occurs, staff are encouraged to find the real reason for the breakdown and correct it without laying blame on anyone. The organization encourages people to continually seek ways to improve processes.

Negative. The organization measures quantity — items produced, numbers served, time spent processing a complaint. Or it may respond to quality or service problems with a crisis response — solving a particular problem, but failing to examine the real causes of the problem. Often management searches for a scapegoat.

1____2____3____4____5____6____7____8____9____10
Negative   Positive

Explanation of Score:

Rewards

Positive. People are rewarded for doing high-quality work. These rewards, which are valued by employees, may include monetary incentives such as bonuses or profit sharing, or may be nonmonetary recognition such as awards, parties, or even management-served breakfasts.

Negative. People do not believe they are given credit or recognition for their work. If a system of rewards is in place, it is commonly viewed with skepticism.

1___2___3___4___5___6___7___8___9___10
Negative   Positive

Explanation of Score:

Performance Review

Positive. Performance review is used primarily as a tool to help plan for the future. Weaknesses are used as opportunities to consider corrective actions. Candid feedback is encouraged from boss to employee, among peers, between work units, and from employee to boss. Performance review is simply a discussion between adults; no one receives a report card with a performance grade on it.

Negative. Performance review is wasteful and demeaning. Quotas are assigned specifying how many employees can receive higher ratings. Individuals, not teams, are rated. Bosses rate subordinates, never the reverse. These number ratings may be used as criteria for determining pay increases. The review process is used primarily to examine past performance rather than as a tool for dealing with the future.

```
1____2____3____4____5____6____7____8____9____10
Negative                                Positive
```

Explanation of Score:

Joy

Positive. People truly enjoy working here. Morale, camaraderie among staff, and fun are a way of life.

Negative. This is a world of False X's. People go through the motions and do what they are asked, but for them it is "just a job."

```
1____2____3____4____5____6____7____8____9____10
Negative                                Positive
```

Explanation of Score:

Once all of the above categories have been discussed, consider the following questions:

- How much support can I expect from senior management if we begin the process of increasing participation?
- What obstacles can I anticipate if we proceed?
- What power do I have to remove obstacles?

From Rick Maurer, *Caught in the Middle: A Leadership Guide for Partnership in the Workplace* (Cambridge, Mass.: Productivity Press, 1992). Copyright © 1992 by Rick Maurer. Permission is granted for reproduction of this page for personal use; re-sale of copies prohibited.

Staff Development Profile

Employee's Name_____ Date_____

Identify specific area of responsibility (such as sales, developing a new program, operating a sophisticated milling maching, etc.):

To the extent possible, rate the employee on factors related to the area of responsibility listed above.

Independence

Rate each item on a scale from 1 to 5. 1 = never, none, or unlike this individual; 5 = always, a lot, very much like this individual

___ Likes to work with little or no supervision.
___ Takes initiative to solve problems.
___ Knows when to ask for help
___ Works well with colleagues.
___ Takes initiative to go beyond what is assigned.

Skills

Indicate which of the following best describes the person's skills to handle this job.

1. Could take on full authority for this particular task today.
2. With minimal training, coaching, or discussion could take on this assignment.
3. With significant training or coaching, could probably take on this assignment.
4. This person could never take over full authority for this assignment.
5. Insufficient information to assess skill level.

Commitment

Assess this employee using a 1 to 5 scale (1 is low; 5 is high).

____ This person meets high standards or sets high standards for his or her own work.

____ This person does whatever it takes to get the job done.

Interpretation

Independence

A high score (20 to 25) indicates the person probably shows sufficient skills to work well on an assignment with little supervision.

Lower scores (1 to 19) indicate that the person may need to be given more independence incrementally. Think of teaching a child to ride a bicycle. You hold tight when the child first gets on the bike and then gradually loosen your grip as you offer suggestions to the rider. Adults often need the same gradual letting-go.

The lower the score, the more help you will need to offer.

Skills

If anyone scored a "5," you might wonder why you aren't taking advantage of this person's skills already; "4" indicates someone who is almost ready to take on the assignment. Consider discussing your expectations with him or her to find out what he or she thinks is needed. This should be an easy task. "3" and "2" require a development plan. "1" is tricky. The person may lack skills or may never have been given an opportunity. As hard as it may be, I encourage you to create a development plan for this person. If you are successful and the person is able to take on even a little more responsibility, you are better off than if you had assumed the person could never do the job.

Commitment

A score of 8 to 10 is a joy to behold. Get out of the way and let these people do their jobs. Scores of 5 to 7 may simply indicate that you need to define the tasks, the importance of the work, and the importance of their participation in this project.

Lower scores (1 to 4) may indicate a serious problem, but assume the best — that given increased responsibility and authority, this person will rise to the challenge. Iincrease responsibility in doses you can stand. Perhaps you might delegate a portion of a task and observe how the employee handles it. If that works, loosen the reins. If increased responsibility doesn't work, look to yourself once again. Ask, "Is there any way in which I might be contributing to the problem?" If you are certain the answer is no, then consider patience, prayer, or personnel action.

An Employee Development Plan

Employee's Name_____ Date_____

Goal

Estimated time for completion

Explanation

STAGE ONE (Orientation):

STAGE TWO (Apprenticeship):

STAGE THREE (Mastery):

What assistance do I anticipate I will need? (To be filled out by employee.)

Resources (books, coaches, training, other units, etc.):

Diagnostic Check for Teams

Mission/Goals

Write a short description (25 words or less) of the team's major responsibilities (its reason for being). You might limit the statement to a particular project, addressing the purpose of the project.

Roles and Responsibilities

Define your major roles in this team (scribe, team leader, liaison to suppliers, etc.).

Define the roles of the other members of the team.

Coordination with Other Teams

Do we actively coordinate our work with the work of our customers and suppliers? Give examples.

Approach

Describe how the team analyzes problems and makes decisions.

Day-to-Day Work

Identify an incident that exemplifies the way in which the team works together day in and day out.

Quality of the Relationships

Respond to each of the following:

• Is it fun working on this team? In what ways?

• Do I feel others listen to me? Do I listen to others? Explain.

• Do I openly encourage others and delight in the successes of team members? In what ways?

• Do we share resources with each other? Describe.

• Do we pitch in to help each other? Give an example.

Interpreting the Assessment

Mission/Goals

The team should know why it exists. All team members should be able to define the mission of the team and state the goals of current projects. In other words, all members of the team should share a common understanding of why they are together and what they are supposed to accomplish.

Too often teams suffer from diffuse or vague goals. Not surprisingly, the work of these teams is inconsistent. One person's top priority item is another's low-priority item simply because they lack a common understanding of the team's direction.

Even slight variations in responses indicate that priorities could be quite diverse. Think of sighting a rifle. An error of mere hundredths of an inch on the sight will cause the bullet to travel far off course.

Roles and Responsibilities

All members of a team must know their respective roles. No basketball coach would ever build a team without identifying forwards, guards, and center, or without being certain that all players know precisely what they are supposed to do on the court.

Roles are not job descriptions. Roles are functional day-to-day "whom should I pass to?" responsibilities. Who is project manager? Who handles budget? Who will coordinate with the office down the hall?

Clear roles and responsibilities increase the chances that people will know what they are supposed to do. Less will fall through the cracks, duplication of effort will be reduced, and turf battles will be diminished.

Coordination with Other Teams

All teams have suppliers and customers. Teams must understand their relationship with other individuals and units. Who must complete work before we can begin? Whom do we serve? Work must be coordinated with these other individuals and teams.

Understanding these relationships helps team members know where to create links with other units to speed up delivery of items or to ensure that the customer will be satisfied with the team's product or service.

Teams must make sure that natural boundaries don't become fortresses that exclude others. When the boundary becomes a fortress, suppliers are transformed into "those damn suppliers" who never get things to us on time, and customers turn into "those jerks who are never satisfied with anything."

Approach

Teams must determine how they will address problems: What approaches will they take in analyzing the causes of a problem, and what steps will they take in determining solutions? How will the team make decisions — by committee, by executive fiat, by the loudest and last to speak, or by a more democratic process?

New teams should create operating norms that guide their actions. Norms or procedures may change, but at least they change by plan rather than by chance. The team might agree to a norm that all meetings start and end on time, or to making sure all team members receive project status as soon as it is posted.

Day-to-Day Work

Teams must look at daily operations and determine where potential problems might occur, because the possibility of missed communication is always high. Identifying potential trouble spots can alleviate many of a team's problems. For example, a salesperson who lacks knowledge of what others on the team are doing may be embarrassed to learn that he has just promised something that he can't deliver, because of heavy demands on stock.

Quality of the Relationship

Getting there should be fun and engaging. People should enjoy working together. If they don't, if people aren't laughing or energetic, your team may have serious problems. Some of these relationship factors are:

- *Fun.* Good teams enjoy themselves. Bad teams don't. Fun does not imply that people are always standing around telling jokes, but people should be smiling, teasing each other occasionally, and seeing the lightness in what they do.

- *Listening.* Team members pay attention to the opinions and feelings of their colleagues and respond to them with respect.
- *Encouraging.* People support and bolster each other and take delight in each other's successes.
- *Sharing resources.* People search for ways to work cooperatively. The new supply of photocopy paper is divided among those who need it and not hoarded by the first to find it.
- *Pitching in.* Team members fill in for others and share some of the burden. Members realize that they all work toward a common goal and it is in all of their interests to see that the work gets done.

Leadership Practices Questionnaire

1. Setting Direction

A. How well do I state and clarify vision, goals, and objectives?

1_____2_____3_____4_____5_____6_____7
Poorly   Very Well

Examples:

What could I do to improve?

B. How well do I lead by example? Do my actions demonstrate a commitment to employee involvement?

1_____2_____3_____4_____5_____6_____7
Poorly   Very Well

Examples:

What could I do to improve?

2. Keeping Others Informed

A. Do I give you helpful and timely feedback regarding your performance?

1____2____3____4____5____6____7
Rarely   Often

Examples:

What could I do to improve?

B. How well do I keep you informed of changes in the business or the work of other units?

1____2____3____4____5____6____7
Poorly   Very Well

Examples:

What could I do to improve?

3. Initiative

A. How well do I encourage you to take risks?

1_____2_____3_____4_____5_____6_____7
Poorly   Very Well

Examples:

What could I do to improve?

B. How well do I use failed risks as learning opportunities (do I punish the risk taker)?

1_____2_____3_____4_____5_____6_____7
Poorly   Very Well

Examples:

What could I do to improve?

4. Support

A. Do I give you sufficient support and encouragement?

1_____2_____3_____4_____5_____6_____7
Rarely   Often

Examples:

What could I do to improve?

B. Does this support feel sincere?

1_____2_____3_____4_____5_____6_____7
Rarely   Often

Examples:

What could I do to improve?

5. Development

A. How well do I provide the help you need to develop skills to do your job?

1_____2_____3_____4_____5_____6_____7
Poorly   Very Well

Examples:

What could I do to improve?

B. How well do I provide support for your career development?

1_____2_____3_____4_____5_____6_____7
Poorly   Very Well

Examples:

What could I do to improve?

6. Coordinating Effort

A. How effectively am I coordinating work within this work unit?

$$1\underline{\hspace{1cm}}2\underline{\hspace{1cm}}3\underline{\hspace{1cm}}4\underline{\hspace{1cm}}5\underline{\hspace{1cm}}6\underline{\hspace{1cm}}7$$
Poorly   Very Well

Examples:

What could I do to improve?

B. How efficiently am I coordinating work between you and our suppliers and customers?

$$1\underline{\hspace{1cm}}2\underline{\hspace{1cm}}3\underline{\hspace{1cm}}4\underline{\hspace{1cm}}5\underline{\hspace{1cm}}6\underline{\hspace{1cm}}7$$
Poorly   Very Well

Examples:

What could I do to improve?

7. Building a Team

How well do I encourage the development of your work team?

1_____2_____3_____4_____5_____6_____7
Poorly   Very Well

Examples:

What could I do to improve?

8. Keeping Yourself Informed

How easy is it for you to criticize me?

1_____2_____3_____4_____5_____6_____7
Impossible   Easy

Examples:

What could I do to improve?

About the Author

Rick Maurer, through his firm, Maurer & Associates, assists managers in building cooperation in the workplace. In his own search for a model that works, he carefully studied leadership practices of managers in a number of well-run organizations — the companies, institutions, government agencies, and other groups that serve their customers, their stockholders, and their employees well.

Based on this study, Rick wrote *Caught in the Middle* and developed a process that can help managers emulate the high-involvement practices of managers in the best-run organizations.

In addition to his consulting practice, Rick teaches in the Leadership Development Program of the Center for Creative Leadership at the University of Maryland, an intensive training program for managers from business, industry, and government.

Based in Arlington, Virginia, Rick has consulted to managers and staff from organizations as diverse as MCI, the government of Guyana, Freddie Mac, the Washington, D.C. public schools, and Pillsbury. He is also a musician and a playwright whose works have been performed in the Washington, D.C. area.

Index

OTHER BOOKS ON EMPLOYEE INVOLVEMENT

Productivity Press publishes and distributes materials on continuous improvement in productivity, quality, customer service, and the creative involvement of all employees. Many of our products are direct source materials from Japan that have been translated into English for the first time and are available exclusively from Productivity. Supplemental products and services include newsletters, conferences, seminars, in-house training and consulting, audio-visual training programs, and industrial study missions. Call 1-800-274-9911 for our free book catalog.

CEDAC
A Tool for Continuous Systematic Improvement
Ryuji Fukuda

CEDAC®, or Cause and Effect Diagram with the Addition of Cards, is a modification of the "fishbone diagram," one of the standard QC tools. One of the most powerful, yet simple problem-solving methods to come out of Japan (Fukuda won a Deming Prize for developing it), CEDAC actually encompasses a whole cluster of tools for continuous systematic improvement. They include window analysis (for identifying problems), the CEDAC diagram (for analyzing problems and developing standards), and window development (for ensuring adherence to standards). Here is Fukuda's manual for the in-house support of improvement activities using CEDAC. It provides step by step directions for setting up and using CEDAC. With a text that's concise, clear, and to the point, nearly 50 illustrations and sample forms suitable for transparencies, and a removable CEDAC wall chart, the manual is an ideal training aid.
ISBN 0-915299-26-7 / 144 pages / $49.95 / Order code CEDAC-BK

The Visual Factory
Building Participation Through Shared Information
Michel Greif

If you're aware of the tremendous improvements achieved in productivity and quality as a result of employee involvement, then you'll appreciate the great value of creating a visual factory. This book shows how visual management can be used to make the factory a place where workers and supervisors freely communicate and take improvement action. It details how to develop meeting and communication areas, communicate work standards and instructions, use visual production controls such as kanban, and make goals and progress visible. Over 200 diagrams and photos illustrate the numerous visual techniques discussed.
ISBN 0-915299-67-4 / 320 pages / $49.95 / Order code VFAC-BK

Manager Revolution!
A Guide to Survival in Today's Changing Workplace
Yoshio Hatakeyama

An extraordinary blueprint for effective management, here is a step-by-step guide to improving your skills, both in everyday performance and in long-term planning. *Manager Revolution!* explores in detail the basics of the Japanese success story and proves that it is readily transferable to other settings. Written by the president of the Japan Management Association and a bestseller in Japan, here is a survival kit for beginning and seasoned managers alike. Each chapter includes case studies, checklists, and self-tests.
ISBN 0-915299-10-0 / 208 pages / $24.95 / MREV-BK

The Idea Book
Improvement Through Total Employee Involvement
Japan Human Relations Association (ed.)

What would your company be like if each employee — from line workers to engineers to sales people — gave 100 ideas every year for improving the company? This handbook of Japanese-style suggestion systems (called "teian"), will help your company develop its own vital improvement system by getting all employees involved. Train workers how to write improvement proposals, help supervisors promote participation, and put creative problem solving to work in your company. Designed as a self-trainer and study group tool, the book is heavily illustrated and includes hundreds of examples. (Spanish edition available.)
ISBN 0-915299-22-4 / 240 pages / $49.95 / Order code IDEA-BK

Kaizen Teian 1
Developing Systems for Continuous Improvement
Through Employee Suggestions
Japan Human Relations Association (ed.)

Especially relevant for middle and upper managers, this book focuses on the role of managers as catalysts in spurring employee ideas and facilitating their implementation. It explains the many aspects of running a proposal program on a day-to-day basis and provides cartoon examples of successful kaizen teian programs in four major Japanese organizations. This concise reference outlines the policies that support a "bottom-up" system of innovation and defines the three main objectives of kaizen teian: to build participation, develop individual skills, and achieve higher profits.
ISBN 0-915299-89-5 / 208 pages / $39.95 / Order code KT1-BK

The Best of TEI
Current Perspectives on Total Employee Involvement
Karen Jones (ed.)

An outstanding compilation of the 29 best presentations from the first three International Total Employee Involvement (TEI) conferences sponsored by Productivity. You'll find sections on management strategy, case studies, training and retraining, kaizen (continuous improvement), and high quality teamwork. Here's the cutting edge in implemented EI strategies — doubly valuable to you because it comprises both theory and practice. It's also amply illustrated with presentation charts. Whether you're a manager, a team member, or in HR development, you'll find The Best of TEI a rich and stimulating source of information. Comes in handy 3-ring binder.
ISBN 0-915299-63-1 / 502 pages / $175.00 / Order code TEI-BK

Individual Motivation
Removing the Blocks to Creative Involvement
Etienne Minarik

The key to gaining the competitive advantage in a saturated market is to use existing resources more efficiently and creatively. Applying this wisdom to a manufacturing company's human resources, this book shows managers how to turn employees' "negative individualism" into creativity and initiative. It describes the shift in corporate culture necessary to enable front line employees to use their knowledge about product and process to the company's greatest benefit.
ISBN 0-915299-86-2 / 176 pages / $24.95 / Order code INDM-BK

Better Makes Us Best
Dr. John Psarouthakis

A short, engaging, but powerful and highly practical guide to performance improvement for any business or individual. Focusing on incremental progress toward clear goals is the key — you become "better" day by day. It's a realistic, personally fulfilling, action-oriented, and dynamic philosophy that has made Psarouthakis's own company a member of the Fortune 500 in just ten years. Buy a copy for everyone in your work force, and let it work for you.
ISBN 0-915299-56-9 / 112 pages / $16.95 / order code BMUB-BK

Productivity Press, Inc., Dept. BK, P.O. Box 3007, Cambridge, MA 02140 1-800-274-9911

The Improvement Book
Creating the Problem-Free Workplace
Tomo Sugiyama

A practical guide to setting up a participatory problem-solving system in the workplace. Focusing on ways to eliminate the "Big 3" problems — irrationality, inconsistency, and waste — this book provides clear direction for starting a "problem-free engineering" program. It also gives you a full introduction to basic concepts of industrial housekeeping (known in Japan as 5S), two chapters of examples that can be used in small group training activities, and a workbook for individual use (extra copies are available separately). Written in an informal style, and using many anecdotes and examples, this book provides a proven approach to problem solving for any industrial setting.
ISBN 0-915299-47-X / 236 pages / $49.95 / Order code IB-BK

40 Years, 20 Million Ideas
The Toyota Suggestion System
Yuzo Yasuda

This fascinating book describes how Toyota generated tremendous employee involvement in their creative idea suggestion system. It reviews the program's origins, Toyota's internal promotion of the system, and examples of actual suggestions and how they were used. This account reveals the role of the Good Idea Club — an autonomous, in-house organization begun by gold-prize award winners, in fostering suggestion-writing ability. Personal accounts and anecdotes flavor the text, address problems encountered and their resolutions, and convey how trust and understanding became key elements of employee/management relationships at Toyota. This case study will give any reader the inspiration to initiate a creative idea suggestion system of their own or significantly revitalize an existing one.
ISBN 0-915299-74-7 / 224 pages / $39.95 / Order code 4020-BK

ALSO FROM PRODUCTIVITY

TEI Newsletter

TEI — Total Employee Involvement — can transform an unproductive, inefficient, even angry work force into a smart, productive, cooperative team. Learn how by reading the monthly TEI . Its articles, interviews, suggestions, and case histories will help you promote a learning organization, activate continuous improvement, and encourage creativity in all your employees. To subscribe, or for more information, call 1-800-899-5009. Please state order code "BA" when ordering.

Productivity Press, Inc., Dept. BK, P.O. Box 3007, Cambridge, MA 02140 1-800-274-9911

COMPLETE LIST OF TITLES FROM PRODUCTIVITY PRESS

Akao, Yoji (ed.). **Quality Function Deployment: Integrating Customer Requirements into Product Design**
ISBN 0-915299-41-0 / 1990 / 387 pages / $ 75.00 / order code QFD

Akiyama, Kaneo. **Function Analysis: Systematic Improvement of Quality and Performance**
ISBN 0-915299-81-X / 1991 / 288 pages / $59.95 / order code FA

Asaka, Tetsuichi and Kazuo Ozeki (eds.). **Handbook of Quality Tools: The Japanese Approach**
ISBN 0-915299-45-3 / 1990 / 336 pages / $59.95 / order code HQT

Belohlav, James A. **Championship Management: An Action Model for High Performance**
ISBN 0-915299-76-3 / 1990 / 265 pages / $29.95 / order code CHAMPS

Birkholz, Charles and Jim Villella. **The Battle to Stay Competitive: Changing the Traditional Workplace**
ISBN 0-915299-96-8 / 1991 / 110 pages paper / $9.95 /order code BATTLE

Christopher, William F. **Productivity Measurement Handbook**
ISBN 0-915299-05-4 / 1985 / 680 pages / $137.95 / order code PMH

D'Egidio, Franco. **The Service Era: Leadership in a Global Environment**
ISBN 0-915299-68-2 / 1990 / 165 pages / $20.95 / order code SERA

Ford, Henry. **Today and Tomorrow**
ISBN 0-915299-36-4 / 1988 / 286 pages / $24.95 / order code FORD

Fukuda, Ryuji. **CEDAC: A Tool for Continuous Systematic Improvement**
ISBN 0-915299-26-7 / 1990 / 144 pages / $49.95 / order code CEDAC

Fukuda, Ryuji. **Managerial Engineering: Techniques for Improving Quality and Productivity in the Workplace** (rev.)
ISBN 0-915299-09-7 / 1988 / 208 pages / $39.95 / order code ME

Gotoh, Fumio. **Equipment Planning for TPM: Maintenance Prevention Design**
ISBN 0-915299-77-1 / 1991 / 320 pages / $75.00 / order code ETPM

Greif, Michel. **The Visual Factory: Building Participation Through Shared Information**
ISBN 0-915299-67-4 / 1991 / 320 pages / $49.95 / order code VFAC

Hatakeyama, Yoshio. **Manager Revolution! A Guide to Survival in Today's Changing Workplace**
ISBN 0-915299-10-0 / 1986 / 208 pages / $24.95 / order code MREV

Hirano, Hiroyuki. **JIT Factory Revolution: A Pictorial Guide to Factory Design of the Future**
ISBN 0-915299-44-5 / 1989 / 227 pages / $49.95 / order code JITFAC

Hirano, Hiroyuki. **JIT Implementation Manual: The Complete Guide to Just-In-Time Manufacturing**
ISBN 0-915299-66-6 / 1990 / 1006 pages / $2500.00 / order code HIRJIT

Horovitz, Jacques. **Winning Ways: Achieving Zero-Defect Service**
ISBN 0-915299-78-X / 1990 / 165 pages / $24.95 / order code WWAYS

Ishiwata, Junichi. **IE for the Shop Floor: Productivity Through Process Analysis**
ISBN 0-915299-82-8 / 1991 / 208 pages / $39.95 / order code SHOPF1

Productivity Press, Inc., Dept. BK, P.O. Box 3007, Cambridge, MA 02140 1-800-274-9911

Japan Human Relations Association (ed.). **The Idea Book: Improvement Through TEI (Total Employee Involvement)**
ISBN 0-915299-22-4 / 1988 / 232 pages / $49.95 / order code IDEA

Japan Human Relations Association (ed.). **The Service Industry Idea Book: Employee Involvement in Retail and Office Improvement**
ISBN 0-915299-65-8 / 1991 / 294 pages / $49.95 / order code SIDEA

Japan Management Association (ed.). **Kanban and Just-In-Time at Toyota: Management Begins at the Workplace** (rev.), Translated by David J. Lu
ISBN 0-915299-48-8 / 1989 / 224 pages / $36.50 / order code KAN

Japan Management Association and Constance E. Dyer. **The Canon Production System: Creative Involvement of the Total Workforce**
ISBN 0-915299-06-2 / 1987 / 251 pages / $36.95 / order code CAN

Jones, Karen (ed.). **The Best of TEI: Current Perspectives on Total Employee Involvement**
ISBN 0-915299-63-1 / 1989 / 502 pages / $175.00 / order code TEI

JUSE. **TQC Solutions: The 14-Step Process**
ISBN 0-915299-79-8 / 1991 / 416 pages / 2 volumes / $120.00 / order code TQCS

Kanatsu, Takashi. **TQC for Accounting: A New Role in Companywide Improvement**
ISBN 0-915299-73-9 / 1991 / 244 pages / $45.00 / order code TQCA

Karatsu, Hajime. **Tough Words For American Industry**
ISBN 0-915299-25-9 / 1988 / 178 pages / $24.95 / order code TOUGH

Karatsu, Hajime. **TQC Wisdom of Japan: Managing for Total Quality Control**, Translated by David J. Lu
ISBN 0-915299-18-6 / 1988 / 136 pages / $34.95 / order code WISD

Kato, Kenichiro. **I.E. for the Shop Floor: Productivity Through Motion Study**
ISBN 1-56327-000-5 / 1991 / 224 pages / $39.95 / order code SHOPF2

Kaydos, Will. **Measuring, Managing, and Maximizing Performance**
ISBN 0-915299- 98-4 / 1991 / 304 pages / $34.95 / order code MMMP

Kobayashi, Iwao. **20 Keys to Workplace Improvement**
ISBN 0-915299-61-5 / 1990 / 264 pages / $34.95 / order code 20KEYS

Lu, David J. **Inside Corporate Japan: The Art of Fumble-Free Management**
ISBN 0-915299-16-X / 1987 / 278 pages / $24.95 / order code ICJ

Maskell, Brian H. **Performance Measurement for World Class Manufacturing: A Model for American Companies**
ISBN 0-915299-99-2 / 1991 / 448 pages / $49.95 / order code PERFM

Merli, Giorgio. **Co-makership: The New Supply Strategy for Manufacturers**
ISBN 0915299-84-4 / 1991 / 224 pages / $39.95 / order code COMAKE

Merli, Giorgio. **Total Manufacturing Management: Production Organization for the 1990s**
ISBN 0-915299-58-5 / 1990 / 224 pages / $39.95 / order code TMM

Mizuno, Shigeru (ed.). **Management for Quality Improvement: The 7 New QC Tools**
ISBN 0-915299-29-1 / 1988 / 324 pages / $59.95 / order code 7QC

Monden, Yasuhiro and Michiharu Sakurai (eds.). **Japanese Management Accounting: A World Class Approach to Profit Management**
ISBN 0-915299-50-X / 1990 / 568 pages / $59.95 / order code JMACT

Nachi-Fujikoshi (ed.). **Training for TPM: A Manufacturing Success Story**
ISBN 0-915299-34-8 / 1990 / 272 pages / $59.95 / order code CTPM

Nakajima, Seiichi. **Introduction to TPM: Total Productive Maintenance**
ISBN 0-915299-23-2 / 1988 / 149 pages / $45.00 / order code ITPM

Nakajima, Seiichi. **TPM Development Program: Implementing Total Productive Maintenance**
ISBN 0-915299-37-2 / 1989 / 428 pages / $85.00 / order code DTPM

Nikkan Kogyo Shimbun, Ltd./Factory Magazine (ed.). **Poka-yoke: Improving Product Quality by Preventing Defects**
ISBN 0-915299-31-3 / 1989 / 288 pages / $59.95 / order code IPOKA

Nikkan Kogyo Shimbun/Esme McTighe (ed.). **Factory Management Notebook Series: Mixed Model Production**
ISBN 0-915299-97-6 / 1991 / 184 / $125.00 / order code N1-MM

Nikkan Kogyo Shimbun/Esme McTighe (ed.). **Factory Management Notebook Series: Visual Control Systems**
ISBN 0-915299-54-2 / 1991 / 194 pages / $125.00 / order code N1-VCS

Nikkan Kogyo Shimbun/Esme McTighe (ed.). **Factory Management Notebook Series: Autonomation/Automation**
ISBN 0-0-56327-002-1 / 1991 / 200 pages / $125.00 / order code N1-AA

Ohno, Taiichi. **Toyota Production System: Beyond Large-Scale Production**
ISBN 0-915299-14-3 / 1988 / 162 pages / $39.95 / order code OTPS

Ohno, Taiichi. **Workplace Management**
ISBN 0-915299-19-4 / 1988 / 165 pages / $34.95 / order code WPM

Ohno, Taiichi and Setsuo Mito. **Just-In-Time for Today and Tomorrow**
ISBN 0-915299-20-8 / 1988 / 208 pages / $34.95 / order code OMJIT

Perigord, Michel. **Achieving Total Quality Management: A Program for Action**
ISBN 0-915299-60-7 / 1991 / 384 pages / $45.00 / order code ACHTQM

Psarouthakis, John. **Better Makes Us Best**
ISBN 0-915299-56-9 / 1989 / 112 pages / $16.95 / order code BMUB

Robinson, Alan. **Continuous Improvement in Operations: A Systematic Approach to Waste Reduction**
ISBN 0-915299-51-8 / 1991 / 416 pages / $34.95 / order code ROB2-C

Robson, Ross (ed.). **The Quality and Productivity Equation: American Corporate Strategies for the 1990s**
ISBN 0-915299-71-2 / 1990 / 558 pages / $29.95 / order code QPE

Shetty, Y.K and Vernon M. Buehler (eds.). **Competing Through Productivity and Quality**
ISBN 0-915299-43-7 / 1989 / 576 pages / $39.95 / order code COMP

Shingo, Shigeo. **Non-Stock Production: The Shingo System for Continuous Improvement**
ISBN 0-915299-30-5 / 1988 / 480 pages / $75.00 / order code NON

Shingo, Shigeo. **A Revolution In Manufacturing: The SMED System**, Translated by Andrew P. Dillon
ISBN 0-915299-03-8 / 1985 / 383 pages / $70.00 / order code SMED

Shingo, Shigeo. **The Sayings of Shigeo Shingo: Key Strategies for Plant Improvement**, Translated by Andrew P. Dillon
ISBN 0-915299-15-1 / 1987 / 208 pages / $39.95 / order code SAY

Productivity Press, Inc., Dept. BK, P.O. Box 3007, Cambridge, MA 02140 1-800-274-9911

Shingo, Shigeo. **A Study of the Toyota Production System from an Industrial Engineering Viewpoint**
ISBN 0-915299-17-8 / 1989 / 293 pages / $39.95 / order code STREV

Shingo, Shigeo. **Zero Quality Control: Source Inspection and the Poka-yoke System**, Translated by Andrew P. Dillon
ISBN 0-915299-07-0 / 1986 / 328 pages / $70.00 / order code ZQC

Shinohara, Isao (ed.). **New Production System: JIT Crossing Industry Boundaries**
ISBN 0-915299-21-6 / 1988 / 224 pages / $34.95 / order code NPS

Sugiyama, Tomo. **The Improvement Book: Creating the Problem-Free Workplace**
ISBN 0-915299-47-X / 1989 / 236 pages / $49.95 / order code IB

Suzue, Toshio and Akira Kohdate. **Variety Reduction Program (VRP): A Production Strategy for Product Diversification**
ISBN 0-915299-32-1 / 1990 / 164 pages / $59.95 / order code VRP

Tateisi, Kazuma. **The Eternal Venture Spirit: An Executive's Practical Philosophy**
ISBN 0-915299-55-0 / 1989 / 208 pages/ $19.95 / order code EVS

Yasuda, Yuzo. **40 Years, 20 Million Ideas: The Toyota Suggestion System**
ISBN 0-915299-74-7 / 1991 / 210 pages / $39.95 / order code 4020

Audio-Visual Programs

Japan Management Association. **Total Productive Maintenance: Maximizing Productivity and Quality**
ISBN 0-915299-46-1 / 167 slides / 1989 / $749.00 / order code STPM
ISBN 0-915299-49-6 / 2 videos / 1989 / $749.00 / order code VTPM

Shingo, Shigeo. **The SMED System**, Translated by Andrew P. Dillon
ISBN 0-915299-11-9 / 181 slides / 1986 / $749.00 / order code S5
ISBN 0-915299-27-5 / 2 videos / 1987 / $749.00 / order code V5

Shingo, Shigeo. **The Poka-yoke System**, Translated by Andrew P. Dillon
ISBN 0-915299-13-5 / 235 slides / 1987 / $749.00 / order code S6
ISBN 0-915299-28-3 / 2 videos / 1987 / $749.00 / order code V6

Returns of AV programs willl be accepted for incorrect or damaged shipments only.

TO ORDER: Write, phone, or fax Productivity Press, Dept. BK, P.O. Box 3007, Cambridge, MA 02140, phone 1-800-274-9911, fax 617-864-6286. Send check or charge to your credit card (American Express, Visa, MasterCard accepted).

U.S. ORDERS: Add $5 shipping for first book, $2 each additional for UPS surface delivery. CT residents add 8% and MA residents 5% sales tax. For each AV program that you order, add $5 for programs with 1 or 2 tapes, and $12 for programs with 3 or more tapes.

INTERNATIONAL ORDERS: Write, phone, or fax for quote and indicate shipping method desired. Pre-payment in U.S. dollars must accompany your order (checks must be drawn on U.S. banks). When quote is returned with payment, your order will be shipped promptly by the method requested.

NOTE: Prices subject to change without notice.